Harvest Entertainment, Inc.

For information, contact:
Harvest Entertainment, Inc.
PO Box 1925
Salt Lake City, Utah 84110-1925
U.S.A.
or **www.actingacrossamerica.com**

FOR SEMINAR BOOKING INFORMATION, CONTACT:
www.actingacrossamerica.com

FIRST EDITION
Designed by David Seppi
Cover designed by Carolyn Richardson, David Seppi and Russ lyman

To my family:

My mother, Janine Virlouvet McGregor,
for her love and always encouraging me to achieve higher goals,

My father, William Stanley McGregor,
for being my light, my mentor, my hero;

My son, Julien, for reminding me what life is for.

ACKNOWLEDGMENTS

Thanks to my friend and attorney, James Leonard, for his unending support, and to Gail Shye, for helping him do so; my casting partner Jeff Johnson, Ed Finch, Camilla Kragius, Gigi Hodges, my Aunt Carol, Mark DeWolfe, Don Shanks, Al Bernstein, Jim Cash, Renee Cash, Carolyn Richardson and Marcia Dangerfield for believing in the book—and in me. To the actors and agents in my beautiful corner of the world—Utah—for helping me to enjoy my career.   To Mike Callahan and many others at Loyola-Marymount University (particularly the Communication Arts department) for a wonderful academic introduction to what would become a career that I love; and to Jenny Burgess for her assistance.

Preface

I didn't set out to write this book.

Over the course of years and years of casting throughout the U.S., I have been asked by plumbers, by waitresses, by lawyers, by students, by hotel employees, by flight attendants, by people of every race, every age, and every physical condition, how one goes about breaking into acting—right where they live.

Few of these aspiring actors had intentions of ever moving to LA or the Big Apple. They had fulfilling lives across our fifty states—but just wanted to act part time. The questions were asked in hotels, while I struggled with luggage, or in the terminals as I rushed to catch a plane, or when I tried to wind down for the day and have a quiet dinner. I wanted to give these people a legitimate resource to consult, but after extensive research, I found none. So *Acting Across America* was created.

Acting Across America is your guide—your resource—to acting regionally. My goal is to educate you, to make you as professional as possible, to answer your questions—and to give you someone to whom you can vent. What you don't find in this book will be answered for you on our website—**www.actingacrossamerica.com**. I want to help you achieve your goals, no matter how big or how small.

Because I want to immerse you in the acting business, I purposely used terms which I don't define within the text-but those terms-and many more-are in the glossary. If you ever encounter a term-a contract-a situation on which you are not clear, please consult me at **www.actingacrossamerica.com**. Don't make what could be a big mistake. Now that you have a coach, you have power behind you! Use it, and good luck!

Love,

Catnie

Table of Contents

Chapter Three: The Unions

Chapter Four: Location Shooting vs. Studio Shooting

Chapter Five: The Scams

Part II: The Audition

Part III: On the Set

Part One: The Business

CHAPTER ONE

The choice: To act or not to act?

Do you know how many actors it takes to change a light bulb? Seven. One to screw it in, and six to say, "I could have done that better."

That may be less of a joke than you think, since many actors got started that way. Have you ever watched a so-so actor on a local commercial and thought, "He got paid for that!" Have you ever seen a movie and thought, "I could have made that character a lot more interesting!" or "I'm better looking than he/she is!" (Yeah.) Then you definitely have the makings of an actor. But remember, even though the will to do it can give you your initial motivation, there are many, many things to consider. The BUSINESS section of this book will give you all of the mundane, but necessary information you need in order to decide whether or not you want to become a film, TV or commercial actor. I'm not going to paint a pretty picture for you. I'll paint an honest one. If you have the grit to absorb the first part of this book, you've got the grit to give acting a whirl. Remember, Picasso honed his skills as a realistic painter before becoming a Surrealist. You, too, need to learn the very basics before you can give Meryl Streep and Al Pacino a run for their money.

Business vs. Art

People who make films, commercials and television shows tell people, quite simply, that they work 'in the business.'

Countless film students, as well as seasoned filmmakers, would certainly bristle at the notion of film being referred to as anything but a creative process. But the sad, realistic truth is that the budget for today's films, TV shows and commercials can be as high as a small country's Gross National Product. Luckily for us, producers who are trying to control the budget, and directors who are trying to adhere to a creative nirvana, find ways to meld their respective interests. You'll learn later in this section how the latter point can affect you directly as a regional actor.

In considering an acting career, you need to think about the impact your decision will make on your present financial status. Only after thinking through the cost of headshots, resumes, acting classes, loss of hours at your job, necessary wardrobe and whatever your own personal necessities are, should you begin to ask yourself if you truly want to act professionally, semi-professionally, or even as a hobby.

If you want to act as a hobby, or semi-professionally, you can do it in any regional market. *Semi-professionally* refers to not making your entire living as an actor. You should take the following expenses into consideration:

1. Headshots and resumes (approximately $200-300)
2. Loss of hours at work
3. Acting classes

Although I can guarantee these costs, there are absolutely no guarantees as to when, or if, you will make back your original investment.

When you begin working professionally as an actor, I would recommend that you meet with an accountant to find out what new write-offs you will have (video rentals, agents' commissions, etc.) as well as how many dependents to claim. Remember, if you work as an actor for one day, even at the minimum pay (scale), there is a good chance that you'll make $1,000. See what options are available to you to make sure that the IRS understands that such a daily rate is a great exception and not the norm, or your salary will be eaten up in taxes!

Headshots and Resumes

(For regional referrals to photographers, labs, printers and make-up artists, check on **www.actingacrossamerica.com**)

Before you can begin to work, you'll need to get a headshot and resume. A headshot is a picture of *you*. You may want to check into getting an agent before you do this, as some agencies have specific guidelines for both of these items. Although it's absolutely true that you must have them, it's not true that either the headshot or the resume needs to be done through the agency. If you find an agency which requires that you use its photographer, you're probably paying way too much and the agency is making a profit on each picture taken.

As you'll see in the chapter about agents, that's not how a legitimate agency keeps its doors open. Your agent may, however, recommend several photographers. I'd suggest calling them, finding out their price, and actually seeing samples of their work first. After all, it is your picture they'll be taking, not your agent's!

You'll find photographers who charge anywhere from $50 to $500 and more for a headshot. Even though I feel that you'll be perfectly capable of finding the right photographer for under $100, make sure you don't just go for the least expensive, as the quality of the photograph may suffer. Your picture could be the first representation of you that the casting director sees.

You've probably bought a car at some point. You go into the dealership with a $15,000 budget, and lo and behold, you find your dream car for that amount. But by the time the salesman explains that the stereo, air conditioning and sunroof aren't included, you're up to $20,000. Watch for hidden costs when having your pictures taken, too. In having your headshots made, these are the costs:

1. The actual photo being taken
2. Hair and make-up (usually for women only)
3. The film
4. The processing
5. The printing of one 8"x10"
6. One 8"x10" negative (sometimes)
7. The reproduction of the shot (at least 100 copies)

You can see that there are several things to ask about. For example, a photographer could charge $30 for a shoot, but each shot which she prints for you costs $80. ASK what's included when a price is quoted to you, and don't go into it until you're comfortable with the agreement. If you're not sure about which photographer to use, besides looking at samples of her work, I'd recommend asking other actors for references - especially in a regional market, where there are only a handful of true headshot photographers.

Some agencies may want two pictures: One dramatic shot, where you'll have a more serious pose; and a lighter shot which may show you smiling. The latter would be used for less serious roles and for commercials. If you can afford two shots, great. If not, at least get one done, since there's nothing you or your agent can do without a headshot.

What is a good headshot?

1. A headshot must look like *you*.
2. There must be something interesting in the eyes.

You may think that the first statement is obvious. It's not. Women, particularly, will often go for 'glamour' shots, with big hair and Tammy Faye make-up. If that's what you look like normally, fine. If it's not, don't waste your money on such a shot, because you'll only be hurting yourself. You must look like your headshot when you walk in the door for your audition!

All film and television acting is conveyed through the eyes. One should be able to look at your headshot and see your soul through your eyes. Look at the upcoming headshots, and you'll see what I mean.

Headshots serve three basic purposes.

1. A headshot can be submitted to a casting director to determine if she wants to see you. If the shot doesn't look just like you -for good or for bad - you're wasting her time and yours.

2. Many casting directors establish a 'callback' pile and a 'pass' pile at the time of the audition. When you walk out of the room, your headshot and resume go into one of those piles. Having a callback pile eliminates the casting director's having to take notes after each audition.

3. At a callback, a director will see people all day long. He may take a note at 9:10 am that he rather liked John Jacobs' audition, but at 9:10 pm, he has no recollection of what John looked like. That's when the headshot is dug out.

Here are several points to remember in order to have a good, professional headshot:

- It should be in black and white, the industry standard. The only time I might recommend otherwise is if one of your biggest assets is your beautiful red hair. Black and white photos read black, brown and blonde hair, but not red.

- Headshots used to be actual headshots - that is, from mid-chest and up. It has become acceptable of late to have three-quarter shots, and sometimes even full-body shots, but remember the eyes!

- It has also become acceptable to have horizontal shots (the picture is printed horizontally instead of vertically).

- Make sure the shot is very clear.

- The headshot which you are submitting should be the same hair color and style that you are actually wearing.

- Even though some actors don't have their name printed on their headshot (because they are always submitted with a resume stapled on), I highly discourage this format. There have been many, many times when a resume has gotten separated from a headshot, and I've had no idea who the actor was. Some agencies request that you have their logo printed onto your headshot. Before you commit to that investment, make sure that you'll be with that agent for awhile.

- Have your headshots properly reproduced. Avoid laser prints in LA or New York, although they are sometimes acceptable in smaller markets.

- A border around your picture is totally optional.

- Avoid wearing busy clothing (checks, dots, etc.) and large jewelry when having your shot done. Remember, we want to see YOU.

Rudee Lipscomb
SAG
D.O.B.: 11-07-86

RuDee Lipscomb (1999 Emmy winner) has a good headshot: It is a clear, no-nonsense shot framed by a clean border. She looks like the beautiful young lady that she is.

Zach's headshot, as you can see, is not a traditional headshot, but is framed a bit wider. It works in that there is a twinkle in the eye and the shot looks like Zach. This is an example of a nice headshot with an interesting border.

ZACH HOPE

Many actors chose to have two headshots: A serious one, and a more commercial one. Often, they will print two resumes as well. If the serious headshot is being sent, they insert the more commercial one into the upper left or right hand corner of the resume, and vice versa.

Now, What to put on a resume?

If you have never acted professionally, do you print your name on the top, and leave the rest blank? NO!

Your resume is the equivalent of your calling card. Would you hand a prospective client a business card full of typos and handwritten notes? Hopefully not. Remember, like your headshot, the resume we see will form our first impression of you and you only make a first impression once. Make sure it's always neat, that there are no typos, and that there is no handwritten information. If you don't have a computer to make resume changes on, you have a friend who does, or there's bound to be a good copy store nearby. Always keep your resume updated on disk.

Your name should be prominent on the top of the page so that we don't have to search for it. Your agency will want you to print its logo on the resume. If you do have an agent, put his phone and fax numbers on the resume, not yours. This is not only a courtesy to your agent, assuring that the casting director goes through him, but it's also more professional. Under your name, state union affiliations (such as SAG, AFTRA, or Actor's Equity). I discourage putting SAG-eligible or AFTRA-eligible, because, as you will see in a future chapter, that means, (in a non-right-to-work state) that you've only done one professional job, and why flaunt that?

I like to see height and weight and hair color, simply because there are times when we're looking to match two actors by height. When this information is on the resume, I can avoid having to track it down through the agent.

Jan Broberg Felt

SAG / AEA

5' 6", 125 lb.
Sea Blue Eyes
Wheat Blonde Hair
Demo Tape Available

FILM:

The Butter Cream Gang II	Supporting	Bruce Neiber/ *Famly Films*
Slaughter Of The Innocents	Featured	James Glickenhaus/ *HBO*
Hope For Troubled Teens	Lead	Blair Treu/ *PBS*
Nadir	Lead	Peter Jazwinski/ *Festival*
Family First	Featured	Ross Ritchins/ *PBS*
Providing In His Way	Lead	Ross Ritchens/ *LDS Church*
Teach The Child	Supporting	Blair Treu/ *LDS Primary*
Sento IT	Lead	Matthew Maddox/ *InfoMedia*
Come Unto Me	Lead	Blair Treu/ *LDS Seminary*

TELEVISION:

Touched By An Angel	Featured	Tim Van Patten/ *CBS Series*
Promised Land	Recurring	Victor Lobl/ *CBS Series*
Taking Of Alta View	Supporting	Peter Levin/ *CBS-MOW*
Siege At Marion	Supporting	Charlie Haid/ *NBC-MOW*
Harmful Intent	Featured	John Patterson/ *NBC-MOW*
Ancient Secrets Of The Bible II	CO-Starring	Tim Nelson/ *CBS Mini Series*
Norman Grayson Story: My Three Wives	Featured	Peter Levin/ *CBS-MOW*
Remember Me	Lead	Kathi Carey/ *PBS Movie*
Death Row	Lead	Kathi Carey/ *PBS Special*
Excaliber	Lead	Rob Bell/ *Infomercial*

THEATER:

Jane Eyre	Jane Eyre	Tim Dietlein/ *Glendale Center, LA*
I Do! I Do!	Agnes	Jane Luke/ *Sundance Theater, UT*
Bus Stop	Grace	Barta Heiner/ *Castle Theater,* "
My Fair Lady	Eliza	Sid Riggs/ *Scera Theater,* "
Company	Amy	Bob Norman/ *Opera West,* "
West Side Story	Anita	Lisa Curtis/ *Bob Carr of Orlando, FL*
Paint Your Wagon	Elizabeth	Vicki Garnick/ *Jackson Hole Playhouse*
Carousel	Julie	Alan Bloomquist/ *Idaho State University*
Sunday In The Park With George	Freida/ Betty	Charles Whitman/ *Brigham Young,* "
Trixie True Teen Detective	Trixie True	Dee Winterton/ *Brigham Young,* "
No No Nannette	Nanette	Ivan Crosland/ *Playmill, Yellowstone*
See How They Run	Penelope	Blenda Horrocks/ *Idaho State University*

COMMERCIALS/ V-O'S/ INDUSTRIALS: *List, Voice Tape, Demo Reel... All Available - Please Ask!*

TRAINING:

BA Theater and Cinematic Arts	Brigham Young University, Suma Cum Laude, 1991
Cold Reading/ Scene Study	Joey Paul, Stephen Mitchell, Catrine McGregor
Audition Technique	Lynn Ellison, Barta Heiner, Ivan Crosland, Charles Metten
Vocal/ Dance	Jan Sullivan, Randy Boothe, Dee Winterton, Peggy Caughney

LANGUAGES/ DIALECTS:
Fluent Spanish, ASL Experience, British, Cockney, Australian, Midwestern and Southern United States

SPECIAL SKILLS/ ABILITIES:
I Sing & Sight-Read Music, Play the Piano, Horseback Ride, Swim, Play Sports, & Love Animals and Kids!

I would advise NOT stating age. Let's say you're 42 and you put that on your resume. The casting director has a role that calls for a 37-year-old. She looks at your shot and thinks you're great for the role until she sees your actual age. I'd like to say that most casting directors would see past that, but it's not always the case.

If you have experience in film, television, commercials, interactive and theater, make headings for each. First, list the name of the project, starting with the latest one. What comes next is optional, but be consistent in your format. Some people put the name of the studio/network/company. I prefer to see who directed the project, and I think it's a great way for actors to go, simply because it can be a springboard for conversation. If I see that you worked on a movie directed by John Doe, whom I respect greatly, it not only gives me something to talk about with you, but tells me that you must be pretty good if John Doe cast you in one of his projects.

If you are truly beginning, and have no credits, don't make any up! Be honest! I don't even object to humor in this case. I personally would not be offended if someone put the above-mentioned headings and, underneath them, a statement such as 'No experience, *yet!*' There is almost nowhere in the country, however, that you can't get experience on stage, whether it's your church, community theater, etc. There is no excuse for not being able to have some working credits on your resume.

After your work experience, put your training. Most casting directors respect actors who take their craft "seriously," and seriously means that they train. . .and continue to train. Whether you're a regional, LA or New York actor, you *must* train. There are always classes out there (see **www.actingacrossamerica.com**). Be careful about who teaches them and about learning bad habits from poor teachers. Just like with local photographers, talk to agents and other actors about the reputation of acting coaches in your area before you invest a large amount of money.

The last item on your resume is Special Skills. List everything that is true about you under this heading. Don't feel silly putting down that you do actually crochet or that you juggle. Who knows, a part may show up that calls for those particular skills, and there probably would be no time to train an actor - bingo! You might get the part. But again, don't stretch the truth, because you could end up with egg on your face.

I once cast a film which called for horseback riding. Judging by the resumes I received, you would have thought our Olympic equestrian riding team consisted of hundreds of people. Almost every resume stated that the actor was an expert rider. When I held the auditions for the role, I gave the actors an address that turned out to be a private home with stables in the back. When the actors realized that the audition was actually going to be held not just on a horse, but a feisty one at that, many recanted their skills. It was much more of a waste of time for them than for me.

From a casting director's point of view, why would I risk my reputation? I know what the role calls for. In this case, poor horsemanship could have consumed hours of filming time and been extremely dangerous.

Resumes don't need to be copied onto a special paper. One agency in LA, however, requires their talent to copy resumes onto a particular shade of green paper. Although the actor may see this as a funny quirk on the part of the agent, it's actually a huge help to the casting director. Remember when I said that most casting directors have a callback pile of headshots? That pile could easily consist of well over a hundred pictures and resumes which need to be sorted BY AGENCY so that the agencies can be notified of callbacks. This process can take forever, with headshots spread all over the floor. The green paper, however, stands out from the rest, and that agency's callback list is quickly put together. I wish all agencies used different colors of paper!

Your headshots and resumes need to be stapled in at least three places, back to back. This means that when I'm looking at your headshot, I should be able to flip it over and see your resume. Make sure the resume is cut down to the same size as the headshot, so that it creates a neat, professional appearance. Headshots are usually 8"x10" and resumes are printed on standard 8 1/2" x 11" paper. Copy stores will cut your resumes down (for a small fee) to fit the 8"x10" photo if you ask. Show them where you want them cut, though, so you have a balanced resume that doesn't cut off any information.

Many actors copy their resume directly onto the back of the headshot. This looks sharp, but unless you're printing up one at a time, I wouldn't recommend it, because as soon as you do a job, that resume becomes obsolete.

TODD A. BRIDGES
SAG & AFTRA

HEIGHT 5'11
WEIGHT 175
HAIR Black
EYES Light Brown

FEATURE FILMS

The Last Stand	Star	Ares Motion Pictures Co.
Diamonds From The Bantus	Star	Pollydor Pictures
The Girl Gets Moe	Guest Star	Jamie Bruce
Pacino Is Missing	Star	Eric M.Galler Twilight Prod.
Busted	Guest Star	Corey Feldman CFI. PM / ENT.
Prisoners of Love	Star	Ace Cruz CHP PRODUCTIONS.
Lunch Time Special	Guest Star	Meno & Soli Moon Fri Skyline
Circle of Pain	Star	Bobby Mardis Fat Chance
She's Out of Control	Star	Stan Dragoti
Sound of Silence	Star	Eric Luzil
Twice Dead	Star	Joe Mose
2021	Star	Sam Watts
Fire Sale	Star	Alen Arkin

MOVIE OF THE WEEK

Police Story	Star	ABC
Circle of Children	Star	ABC
Katherine	Star	NBC
Killing Affair	Star	ABC
High School U.S.A	Star	Glenn Wilder

MINI SERIES

Roots	Star	Gelbert Moss

TELEVISION SERIES

FISH	Star	Danny Arnold
Diff'rent Strokes	Star	Gerien Keith
The Waltons	Star	ABC
Here's Boomer	Star	NBC
L. A Heat	Star	PM Entertainment

TELEVISION SHOWS

The Judge	Star	ABC
Lassie	Star	Al Burton
Barney Miller	Star	Danny Arnold
Love Boat	Star	Richard Kinon
Little House on the Prairie	Star	Michael Landon
CIRCUS OF THE STARS	STAR	ABC
BATTLE OF NETWORK STARS		

Todd's resume is good. You can clearly see what he's done: It's sharp, it's accurate, it's to the point.

The cost of acting

"Acting is not an important job in the scheme of things. Plumbing is."
·Spencer Tracy

Spencer Tracy

The financial costs of acting are by all means not the only costs. Take a long, hard look at the emotional risks at hand before you commit to entering into the business.

When you become an actor, you're baring yourself to the world. By drawing on your emotional make-up to make a scene real, you are sharing some deep secrets.

So, imagine you're going to an audition where you dig into the depths of your soul to give a powerful read. You're shaking when you leave the audition. You nailed that part. The casting director was in tears. You get home, and you call your mom. This is it! You're sure you got this one! One day goes by, two days go by, three days go by - no word. You call your agent and find out that you're not even getting a callback! What happened?

You can't analyze a situation like that, because any number of things could have happened, none of which were within your control. The part might have been written out. You were up for the part of the mom, and you just don't physically match the kid who's the lead, etc.

Are you prepared to face rejection over and over and over again? Are you prepared to make the audition the job, with getting the part being icing on the cake? Are you prepared to tell everyone you're an actor and get asked constantly why they don't see you on TV or on the big screen? Do you have an answer for your spouse who wants to know why you haven't replaced the money in your savings account that you took out for your headshots? Are you ready to be submitted for the part of a radish in a salad commercial? I guess, in short, the question is simply: Is it what you truly want, and are you ready for all it takes?

If you can honestly answer 'yes,' then you're also ready to face what will be some of the most exhilarating, satisfying moments of your life. I think politics is probably the only other career that gets into your blood as much as the entertainment field. And are they really that different?

As fulfilling and satisfying as an acting career may be, it can also be

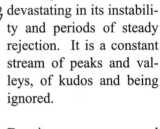

devastating in its instability and periods of steady rejection. It is a constant stream of peaks and valleys, of kudos and being ignored.

Despite your personal traumas, know that most professionals have no tolerance for drugs and alcohol on the set. When a film crew gathers to work, not only are millions and millions of dollars at stake, but there are human lives at risk. Keep your bad habits to yourself at home, and show no sign of them in any way at an audition or on the set.

Before absolutely deciding to go into this line of work, think not just twice, but three and four times about the emotional toll it may take on you. Remember, although acting may be a passion of yours, it's not curing cancer. Keep it all in perspective.

Cami McCroskey's break!

I was once casting an IMAX movie in the Ozarks. The film carried the viewer through several generations of a family, which was a casting nightmare, especially since we were doing almost all of the casting locally. There was a part which called for a beautiful, pure, seventeen-year-old woman to be a bride. I had the additional constraint of having to cast someone who wore a size 6, since the costume designer had already acquired the spectacular wedding dress which would be used in the film.

I had seen everyone there was to see in southern Missouri or so I thought. I had narrowed the role down to two women, but instinctually felt that neither was right. The three of us had been waiting for the director for almost an hour when he called to say that he was stuck on a location scout, and would be a while longer. I was casting in the executive offices of the IMAX theater, so in order to appease the actors, I went downstairs to the concession stand to get them a Coke. While there, I saw a girl standing in line whose smile was radiant. She had a warm, sweet aura about her and, at a glance, looked like she'd fit into the wedding dress. When I approached her, I found out that she was a local (a rarity in Branson) and on a double-date to see a movie. She had done high school theater and was thrilled to audition.

When the director got there, he had three actresses to see, but I knew who'd get the part. And when my new discovery, Cami McCroskey, blushed at just the right moment during the audition, she had won the director's heart and the part. Cami is one of the sweetest girls I've met. I wish her continued success!

In order to stay ready to work, you will need to surround yourself with a strong support system, one you can trust. One such group is often your acting class. A good acting class becomes more than a learning environment it becomes one of trust, of love, of peeling off layers, of friendship. Draw on family, on friends, on fellow-actors to stay positive.

And don't compromise your morals or ethics for an acting job. Understand that if you will not say certain words, or participate in violent films, or films with nudity, you will limit the projects on which you can work; but that in no way means that you should do anything that you are uncomfortable with. It's your legitimate choice. Please let your agent know what your parameters are, so you won't be submitted on any such project. The projects will come and go, but you'll always have to live with yourself.

Don't forget who you are. No character could ever be created that is more interesting than a whole human being, and you have that whole human being to work with! Use every ounce of experiences, humor, darkness, fears and quirks that are YOU!.

Learning the Lingo

Henry Fonda told of the first time he was given a film script, and was somewhat alarmed by a character named 'Dolly' who appeared throughout the film, in almost every room, yet never spoke.

"Bob crosses to the door and walks into bar," read the puzzled Fonda. "Dolly goes with him." At last, he went to the director. "Who is Dolly?" he demanded. "If she doesn't say anything. Why include her?"

The director laughed and accompanied Fonda to the set, where the camera was positioned on board a low trolley which traveled alongside the actors as they moved about the set.

"That," said the director, "is a dolly."

Here's a comment which could easily be said to you, the actor, on a set:

"As the 2nd, I'm supposed to tell you that the honeywagon is over there. That's where your sides are, too. We're not really sticking to the call time, because the DP isn't feeling well. So we're just dealing with second team right now. Do you know where craft service is?"

Sound like a foreign language?

Every business has its terminology, and the film and TV business is no exception. Such terminology becomes second nature to professionals, and makes novices stand out like a sore thumb. The glossary at the back of this book can help you become more familiar with the lingo. Please read it.

Children as Actors

There are many parents out there who thoroughly dislike me. Here's why.

I will never let the parents come into an audition with their child for several reasons. The most obvious is that we need to see how well the child can take direction without the parent in the room. It's usually an asset for the child to not have the parent coaching and smiling and being cute so that the child can actually audition, instead. My main reason for not letting the parent in, however, is that I will usually not audition a child who doesn't want to be there. I always talk to the kids before I audition them. I get a feel for who they are and what they like to do. Children haven't yet developed the horrid ability to mask their emotions, so it's pretty easy to tell how willing they are to be there. If a child would much rather be out playing baseball than coming to an audition on a beautiful Saturday afternoon, let him do so.

Please do not force a child to become an actor. Childhood disappears too quickly as it is without being pushed into a world of competition, politics and situations that are, potentially, even worse.

On the other hand, if your child wants to act, you've got a different set of choices. As a parent, are you prepared to incur the costs mentioned earlier? Are you able to take your child to auditions at the drop of a hat? If your child doesn't read yet, are you prepared to teach her the lines? And if she does read, are you prepared to take the time to run lines with her?

The child actor's career is not much different from the adult's. Once committed to a professional career, the relationship to the agent, the basic union rules, the auditioning process all remain the same. Many states have labor laws that limit the child's working hours, and SAG and AFTRA also have such rules which must be adhered to. If your child is working during school hours, the production company must furnish a competent set teacher. The child is 'in school' between scenes.

SAG and AFTRA have guidelines which they encourage families to follow regarding the use of the child's pay. Such rules dubbed the 'Jackie Coogan' rules are, in my opinion, not nearly stringent enough. Parents are not obligated to set aside a certain amount of the child's money for the future unless the production company initiates such an agreement. Many child actors have been left penniless as adults because of their parents' misuse (or use!) of the money. I would encourage all parents with acting children to put at least 75% of all monies earned into a savings account of some sort for the child to use at a later time.

The remaining 25% of that money can be used to pay for headshots and resumes, gas to go to auditions and any other hard costs associated with the career.

I have extremely mixed emotions about children taking acting classes. Many children's acting classes are taught by incompetent coaches who have an amazing ability to stifle every wonderful natural instinct that a child has. I've seen child after child turned into obnoxious auditioning robots by bad acting teachers.

I've cast many movies with children in the lead, and have almost never hired a child who had any previous experience and especially, previous training. 'Fresh' children have no preconceived notions, and haven't been taught how to *be cute*.

Remember, children are people and are actually quite good at voicing their likes and dislikes. If acting becomes stressful to your child, allow him to pull out and pursue a child's life. We're only children once - and for such a short time.

Is acting open to all ages, races, and physically challenged people?

The answer to the above question is an unequivocal YES!

Retire at 65? That's ridiculous! I still had pimples at 65!
-George Burns

The studios and networks like to see films cast with a real mix of people -the same mix that would be found in the real world. Use that! There are thousands of actors in their 20's and 30's, but far fewer in their 70's and 80's. Pearl Leidy is an actress who started her acting career in her 70's! And she now has an extensive resume, having played the 'cute old lady' in many movies, TV shows and commercials. Fabulous character actor Sidney Greenstreet's first role was at the age of 61 in the film *The Maltese Falcon*! These opportunities are even more open to you if you are a regional actor, and are somewhat of a minority in that area.

Curley Green is a Utah actor who works all the time. Part of the reason is, of course, that he's a wonderful actor. The other is that he's black in a community that is hugely blonde-haired and blue-eyed. Curley's line to directors coming in from LA is: "There are 12 black actors in Utah, and I play 8 of them."

A good line, but sad to say, there's a lot of truth to it.

The same holds true for physically challenged actors. SAG has a listing of actors with disabilities, and producers try to employ them whenever the opportunity arises.

Use your assets! Your unusual traits might even help you get in the door in certain circumstances. But remember, it will be *your ability as an actor* that will get you the role.

What jobs are there for actors?

If you truly want to be an actor, you also must be a director and a marketing whiz.

You will need to become a director to give a great audition. And to simply get jobs, you'll have to learn how to package and present yourself as a valuable commodity. "Not me," you say. "I have an agent." But as far as really pushing your career, an agent and a quarter will get you a phone call. Agents have too much to do to really be concerned about your career. And until you've got experience under your belt, you won't be able to get a good manager. So who's left? You? Your spouse? Your friend? Probably you. So, where do you start?

First of all, what jobs are available for actors on a set?

Actor:

- A person cast in a project who has either dialogue or very specific direction.

- **How do you get the job?** Read this book.

- **Pay:** If SAG or AFTRA, from union scale on up (I'm purposely not giving the scale amount, as it changes as dictated by the SAG contract), plus residuals. If non-union, from free on up.

stunt Person:

- A person who does stunts. Anything even remotely dangerous can   qualify as a stunt. The stunt person is often doubling for an actor. It's more common to see a stunt person who acts than an actor who does stunts. It is a dangerous job which pays well.

- **How do you get the job?** Usually through the stunt coordinator, seldom through the casting director. Because so much is at risk, stunts are hard to get into. Get to know the right people either while working as an extra, or by pursuing the stunt coordinator via letter, phone or e-mail.

- **Pay:** If SAG or AFTRA, union scale on up, plus adjustments or bumps (increases in base pay based on how dangerous and complicated the stunt is) and residuals. If non-union, free on up.

Voice over:

- This is not done on the set, but in post-production. Voice work can be narration, or background voices (known as ADR or looping).

- **How do you get the job?** Through the casting director or voice casting director.

- **Pay:** If SAG or AFTRA, from union scale on up, plus residuals. If non-union, free on up.

stand-in:

- A person hired to replace an actor when the cameras aren't rolling. After doing a scene, actors leave the set to rest, for wardrobe changes, for touch-ups in make-up, etc. The stand-in steps in and walks through the next scene so the camera movement and lighting can be set. A stand-in must be the same weight and height and coloring as the person they're standing in for. They must also be wearing the same color.

- **How do you get the job?** Most stand-ins are hired by the casting director or extras coordinator. Big stars sometimes have their own stand-ins.

- **Pay:** Usually not union regulated. $100-150 per day.

Photo double:

- A person who doubles for an actor in shots that are obscure enough for the real actor to not be identified (i.e. driving shots). Must look like the actor.

- **How do you get the job?** Usually, through the casting director or extras coordinator. Again, some big stars have their own photo double. The same person can be both the stand-in and photo double for one actor.

- **Pay:** Usually not union regulated. $100-150 per day.

Extra:

- A person who is in the background of the scene being filmed and has no lines.

- **How do you get the job?** Through the extras coordinator.

- Pay: If union, scale on up. If non-union, usually $30-$80 per day.

What are the different kinds of projects?

1. Movies
2. TV episodic (series & sitcoms)
3. Movies of the Week (MOW's)
4. Soaps
5. Interactive (CD-ROM)
6. Commercials (national, regional, local)
7. Industrials (training, theme parks, etc.)
8. Infomercials

OK, those are the jobs. There's plenty of work. Now, how do you get it?

Marketing yourself:

The most obvious way to get an audition is to have your agent (if you have one) submit your headshot and resume to the casting director. If you don't have an agent, and you know where the casting is taking place, you can send a headshot and resume along with a cover letter.

There are also on-line companies which have many of the top casting directors using their web casting. This usually consists of your headshot(s), resume, and a short scene which the casting people can watch. It's an interesting concept, and from a casting director's point of view, could eliminate some cattle calls - I would at least have an idea of what your general type is. But film and TV will always be cast, ultimately, in person.

You'll see in future chapters that well over 90% of your audition is about your attitude and the way in which you present yourself in person. In that light, there are inherent problems with on-line casting from a casting person's perspective. We will never know how current the database is. Has that woman cut her hair? Is his hair still bleached blond? Has she put on thirty pounds? We have none of these concerns when we see you in person.

The well-established and, of course, well-respected Academy of Motion Picture Arts and Sciences (the organization which brings you the Academy Awards) has always put out a series of books called the *Academy Players Directory* which shows your picture and lists who your agent or manager is. Anyone can pay to be in it, and anyone can pay to buy the books. The Academy is now putting actors' information on the Internet.

Just like any other burgeoning field, Internet casting will have a deluge of new companies jumping on the bandwagon. Be aware of who you're handing your money over to.

You can find out about projects that are being done through the film and television industry trade journals known as 'the trades' (see **www.actingacrossamerica.com**); specifically, *The Hollywood Reporter* and *Variety*, which come out daily. Journals such as *Backstage West* also offer a lot of valuable information for actors. The trades are geared more to film and TV executives than they are to actors, but they each have a weekly breakdown of projects in preparation and projects in pre-production. These listings give you the name of the project, the stars, the producer, the director, the writer, and often, the casting director. It will also tell you where the project is going to be shot. There's a great way for you to market yourself, especially if you're a regional actor and there's a project coming to your area. You'll see in Chapter 4 why it is such an asset for producers to hire local talent.

Backstage West is geared more to actors and gives breakdowns on all types of projects, including student films, which are a great way to get experience on film and to meet budding filmmakers.

Although the latter journals give information mainly about projects in LA, you can certainly contact universities and colleges in your area to see if they have a film department. If they do, get your headshot and resume to them for future projects. There is no pay on student films, but the experience is invaluable. Most student films will also provide you with footage of your role so that you can start building a reel. Local newspapers also post notices about plays that are being cast, and always have extensive coverage about movies or TV shows coming into your area.

Since agents are primarily concerned about their 10% commission, you can understand why they would not steer you in this direction even though it is great for your career.

Interactives (CD-ROMs) are a relatively new technology. It has only been recently that the quality of interactives has warranted using professional actors, requiring that producers become SAG or AFTRA signatories (see Chapter 3). Because the technology is so relatively new, the doors are not as closed to actors as they are at studios or networks. Your local library's reference desk should help you track down the names and addresses of interactive producers, or you can find them on-line. Copy the information and send in a headshot and resume to the director of creative affairs. At interactive companies, I would recommend following through with a phone call. They will probably be quite open to telling you what the status of their projects are and who actually casts the actors.

I am the production consultant/casting director for Microsoft/IMAAGE, Utah. They are the creators of *Links* and the *Tex Murphy* detective series. I have cast the likes of James Earl Jones (*Star Wars*), Michael York (*Austin Powers*) and Tanya Roberts (*That 70's Show*) in their projects but I have also cast dozens of regional actors. Interactive is a wonderful venue for actors.

Then, there's personal networking. With commercials, industrials, and infomercials, you can often get work because you know the president of the company, or an executive at the ad agency. Get a good filing system together to keep track of the cards of people you meet. Make an effort to stay in touch with these people so that you keep a positive business relationship running. You'll never know when one of them will need an actor for a training video or infomercial.

Keep in mind that all of these open doors are just that. You can only get the job if you are good at what you do. And that only comes from experience, a lot of hard work, and *training, training, training*!

Craig White's break!

Craig was a working musician who had been in an on-going play as a child. Acting had never been a priority, but when he and a friend heard that the mini-series The Blue and the Grey was being shot nearby, they went to the cattle call. And a cattle call it was. Thousands of people showed up for a chance at a part in a big TV project! Discouraged, Craig wanted to leave, but his friend encouraged him to stay since they'd driven quite a ways to the audition.

After a long wait, Craig and his friend finally auditioned. They must have done well, because of all the people who showed up that day, Craig and his friend were the only two people to get cast! Now, friends have to endure endless rewinding and fast-forwarding before Craig finds his one scene but what does he care? He's still getting residuals.

Craig is still acting, and he's also a producer.

What can you expect as an actor, whether you're regional or in LA?

If I could really answer that question, I would have made my fortune picking winning lottery numbers.

You should expect nothing. You should, however, set goals for yourself and try to stick to them as much as you can, while allowing yourself leeway and flexibility along the way.

Regionally:

If you are reading this book to become a regional actor, your steps should be somewhat as follows:

1. Start studying. Take classes. Audition for local plays. Never stop this process.

2. Check out the market: How much is done in your area? Talk to your area's film commission (see **www.actingacrossameri ca.com** and the Appendix).

3. Where is the nearest agency? Is there more than one? Check out all of the agencies and find out if they're taking new clients.

4. Have your headshots taken. Print up your resume.

5. Commit to an agent in your area. If there is no agent, start pursuing the venues mentioned earlier. MARKET YOURSELF!

6. You could start working within a week, or it could take a couple of years. You could make a substantial amount of money, or you could make nothing. The gamble is all part of the adrenaline rush!

If you're planning an eventual move to LA or New York to pursue your acting, try to get into SAG or AFTRA while you're still in a regional market. It will be much easier there than in LA or New York, especially if you live in a right-to-work state (see **www.actin-gacrossamerica.com** and the Appendix).

Los Angeles:

Although there are far more projects being done in LA than anywhere else, it can be much harder to get in the door there. Why? There's a lot more competition. Unless you are breathtakingly good-looking or are already well-known in another field (athletics, for instance) it will be extremely hard to get into SAG or AFTRA, and therefore, almost impossible to get an agent. Agents are flooded with actors - *many of them name actors* - looking to get an agent or, more likely, to change agents. They have such a wide variety of union actors to work with that you probably will never make it past the receptionist until you are at least a member of SAG or AFTRA. That's because almost all projects done are SAG or AFTRA.

After getting your headshot and resume, and getting some training, you MUST focus on getting into the union if you don't live in a right-to-work state. In Chapter 3, I carefully outline the three ways in which you can do this.

Once you are in the union, the battle begins. I'm sorry to liken an acting career to something as hideous as war, but the analogy has been made by more than one Vietnam vet - and not in a kind way. Many have stated that acting is more cut-throat than war. Your armor is your passion, your professionalism, your strength, and your ability to trudge on, and enjoy the voyage.

Don't think getting into SAG or AFTRA will automatically get you an agent. It won't. And don't think getting an agent will automatically get you work. It probably won't. But it's a start.

Whether you're in LA, New York, Minnesota or South Dakota, I can only emphasize two things to get ahead: ***train, and market yourself.***

Preparation

Dustin Hoffman and Sir Laurence Olivier starred opposite each other in the film *Marathon Man,* and they approached their roles quite differently. Being a method actor, Hoffman turned up on set looking exhausted. When Olivier inquired why he looked that way, Hoffman explained that he had kept himself awake since the day before in preparation for a scene to be shot that day in which his character is in the same predicament. Olivier was not impressed. "My dear boy," he said, "if you learned to act, you wouldn't have to stay up all night."

There are almost as many acting styles as there are actors. As a casting director, I don't quite feel qualified to tell you how to prepare for an audition from an actor's standpoint. But I can tell you what preparation pays off at an audition. Besides training in classes, you can also read wonderful books about acting technique and actors' personal stories.

Nepotism

Albert Einstein was being shown around the Warner studio by one of the executives when they ran into Jack Warner. "This is the great Professor Einstein," said the exec, "the man who discovered the Theory of Relativity."

Mr. Warner smiled. "I've proved a theory of relatives, too," he said.

"Really?" asked Einstein, intrigued. "Yeah," Warner quipped, "don't hire 'em."

You've probably heard that in the film business, it's not *what* you know, it's *who* you know. There's a lot of truth to that. Although, once you know *someone*, you still have to know *something*.

Unlike most businesses, there's little or no room for training people on a film or TV project. You get hired, you work independently twelve to fourteen hours a day, the film shoots, and it's over. That's the case for actors, but it's also the case for crew members. When we hire you or cast you, we have to know you can pull your own weight. We only know you can pull your weight if we've seen you do it before, either on the job or at an audition. Therefore, when another project comes up, and you again do a good job, you'll continue to work within those same circles. The hard part is breaking into the circle in the first place. Understand though, this sort of nepotism is not mean-spirited, but a leg-up earned by your good work.

CHAPTER TWO

THE AGENT

A verbal contract isn't worth the paper it's written on.
-attributed to sam Goldwyn

There are two types of representation for actors: Agents and managers. Agents represent many clients at once, and you tend to be one of many. They don't have time to really guide your career, and are mostly concentrating on their commission. A manager, on the other hand, may take more money from you, but may also be more concerned about the overall picture in regard to your career. He or she is more likely to be interested in developing your career than an agent would be. For example, if someone wanted you to donate your talents to a wonderful educational project which would guarantee you publicity, your manager might be interested because of the long-term effects of such a project. Your agent would probably only see the bottom line: 10% of nothing is nothing. So he would probably pass.

How do you get an agent?

If you're in LA or New York, agents' names are easy to come by, but finding a good agent, and one that will take you on as a client, may be more of a challenge. Besides references from friends, and the Yellow Pages, you can contact SAG about a list of SAG-franchised agents. A SAG-franchised agent is somewhat supervised by SAG in that they must adhere to several regulations, such as keeping an account separate from the general operations account for talent monies. I would never recommend going with a non-SAG-franchised agency if in LA or New York. In the regional markets, it is quite a different story and some states have no SAG agencies whatsoever.

You can find out where the agencies in your state are by calling your area's film commission (see **www.actingacrossamerica.com** and the Appendix). Keep in mind the film commission may not know who's franchised and who's not, so it's up to you to know how to screen agencies. There are many states that have absolutely no SAG-franchised agencies, and that can be fine. Just know what to look for. At the end of this chapter, I've provided you with an actual checklist of questions to ask potential agents.

It takes no special training to be an agent. Literally anyone can open their doors and call themselves an agent even if they know nothing about the business. It's a sad state of affairs, but a very real one. And sadder yet, many of these so-called agencies don't have any interest in really learning how things are supposed to be done. They see the masses of people wanting to be actors and prey on them.

Don Shanks, the Native American co-star of *Grizzly Adams*, and Michael Myers in *Halloween V,* moved away from Los Angeles in order to raise his family in a calmer environment. A local agent contacted him over and over again to get him as a client for projects being done in his adoptive state. Being a very kind person, Don agreed. The new enthusiastic agent subscribed to the trades and soon informed him that she had submitted his headshot and resume to many projects listed in pre-production. A bit leery, Don asked what the projects were and who was directing them. The agent replied that she had a complete list, as she'd addressed all of the envelopes to the director. "And the strange thing is," she said, "about 50% of them are being directed by the same person." Keeping in mind that a director has to give at least six months to a year of his life to a project, Don was intrigued and concerned about the agent's statement.

Don Shanks

"Who would that be?" he asked.

"I don't know his full name," she replied, "they only gave his initials: TBD."

TBD stands for 'To Be Determined.'

These are the same agencies which will most likely want you to use their photographer, their lab, their make-up artist, and take their classes. If agents aren't focusing 100% on making commissions, or in other words, *working on your behalf,* they're not doing their intended job.

How much should you pay an agent?

First of all, remember that your agent stays in business because of his 10% commissions. Pay your commissions in a consistent and timely manner.

Agents can only take 10% of SAG or AFTRA contracts. They can not take more. This means if you get a role in a SAG or AFTRA project and your agent only negotiates the base union rate (or scale), you can not legally pay your agent. In order to get paid, they would have had to negotiate (at the least) scale and an additional 10% commission. This is commonly referred to as 'scale plus ten.' If your agent negotiates a much higher amount, then it is negotiable on a case by case basis as to whether or not another 10% would be added. For example, if your agent gets you $3,000 per week, unless she negotiates 10% above and beyond that, you would owe your agent $300 per week. Your net would then be $2,700, less taxes.

Agents are never paid a salary by you, nor is there a sign up fee, or a charge to the actor for mailing or delivery of your headshots for project submissions. If an agent is requiring any of these fees, turn and run.

Regional agents will often get you work on local commercials, infomercials and industrials that are non-union, which is fine if you're not a member of SAG or AFTRA. On many of these contracts, they'll bill the client your whole amount plus a 10% commission. When the check comes to them, they take the 10% from your check. For example, your agent negotiates $500 for you. They bill the production company $550. The agent takes the $50 above and beyond the base pay, then takes $50 from your $500. Again, know up front what the arrangement is.

Most agents want your paycheck to go to them instead of to you so that they are guaranteed to get their commission in a timely manner. Many agents also say it's actually an asset to you, because it's the only way that they can efficiently keep track of whether or not you've been paid. Sounds good for them, but what guarantees do you have that you will then get your 90% in a timely manner? *None.*

In order for a production company to pay the agent instead of paying you, they will require a check authorization form, which is a form signed by you, authorizing your check to go directly to the agency. Be careful with these. Agents have been known to get an actor to sign one (supposedly for one specific project), then use that same authorization for all future projects. Before signing such an authorization, I would ask fellow-actors about the agent's reputation for handling talent money.

When I get an acting job, when can I expect my check?

If it is a union job, you must be paid within ten days. If it's a non-union job, good luck. It can take ad agencies and production companies up to six months to pay. Again, ask up-front so that there are no surprises. If you do not get a check, or the amount is wrong, it is part of your agent's job to correct the problem.

Do I sign a contract when I get an agent?

The answer to that is maybe *yes*, maybe *no*. Some agents require it, some don't. And as the Goldwynism at the beginning of this chapter indicates, it doesn't matter anyway. From your standpoint, it will not guarantee you more work. And from the agent's standpoint, he's probably fully aware that the contract is null and void if he does not get you work within any thirty-day period. If you have an agent that sends you out enough that you get work every thirty days, trust me, you don't want to change agents anyway.

What are my agent's obligations to me?

To send you out for roles that are right for you, to follow up on such auditions, to negotiate the best possible deal and billing, and to make sure that you get the right amount of money in a timely manner. Agents need to keep you apprised as to whether or not they have enough of your headshots and resumes to work with. Agents are never authorized to pass (or say no) on a role - any role - without first consulting you.

What are my obligations to my agent?

Several things. It's important that he always have an adequate number of updated headshots and resumes, that you pay him your commissions, that you be professional at auditions and on the set, and that you only have one agent at a time. As usual, there are several exceptions.

Some working actors may have a theatrical agent who represents them for film and television, and a separate commercial agent for commercials. It's in the actor's best interest that each agent be aware of the other.

Another exception: In many of the major markets, like San Francisco and New York, it is allowable for actors to freelance with different agents before signing a contract. Never try to secretly sign with two agents at once. If a casting director gets a submission for the same person from two different agencies, what do you think will happen? Speaking strictly for myself, that person is instantly eliminated from the running. Why? I don't want to be in the middle of a fight between two agents if that actor should ever get the role.

Managers

Managers usually represent anywhere from one to ten clients, so that they have time to truly guide the career of all of their clients. Because managers are not regulated by the unions, they sometimes take up to a 25% commission (although 15% is the norm) and sometimes even charge a monthly fee. It is also typical for a manager to require reimbursement for postage, phone calls and other out-of-pocket expenses.

If you are just beginning your acting career, think twice about having a manager. If you are just starting, it would be hard to understand why a good manager would want to take you on as a client anyway. At this phase of your career, if you had a manager, it would probably be a spouse, friend or parent. It's wonderful to have the wholehearted support of these people, but at the same time, do they know enough to help your career, or is there the risk of them accidentally harming it? Be clear about financial arrangements in these situations, as well. Money has a funny way of creating bad situations between even the best of friends.

Are there any other people in an actor's support team?

Besides having an agent and manager, actors truly making a living at acting may also have a publicist, a lawyer, and a business manager.

- A publicist usually represents many clients, and is on a flat retainer, plus expenses. They are well-connected (you hope!) to producers of TV entertainment news shows, publishers of magazines such as *People*, and the organizers of film festivals and celebrity events. Their job is to make your name known to the public for good, and sometimes, even for bad. Publicists, like naughty children, will sometimes seek negative attention from the press, since they feel that any attention is better than no attention. Most often, they deter negative press.

  Publicists are responsible for making otherwise unknown people household names. A good publicist can be worth his weight in gold but not until he has something to work with.

- Lawyers also come into play later in the game, since their contribution is only required for complex contracts. Lawyers work either on a retainer or a project-percentage basis.

- Business managers are the ones you usually only hear about when they've taken all of someone's money, either by actual embezzlement or just poor money management. Many actors have all of their checks sent to their business managers, who in turn pay all of their bills and make investments. It's a great arrangement when it's working and a nightmare when it's not. Business managers usually work on a percentage basis (5%) of earnings.

Before you sign with an agent, meet with every agency you can in your community and ask them the following Test Questions. It will give you a good indication of the level of their knowledge and professionalism, which is what you're looking for in someone who is going to represent you.

The Agent Test

1. Are you SAG-franchised?

Know this answer before you go in. You can find out from your local SAG representative who is or is not franchised. In many right-to-work states, non-SAG-franchised agents still negotiate SAG deals. It's not the way the union likes to work, but if there are no SAG-franchised agents in the area, there's not much they can do. In a non-right-to-work state, however, you need to be with a SAG-franchised agent in order to get SAG work.

The answer to this question is a simple *yes* or *no*. If the agent has trouble answering, you can be pretty well-assured that he doesn't know much about the industry.

2. What would I need to join this agency?

The agent should tell you that she will need headshots and resumes. This is absolutely correct. Telling you that they will set up a photo-shoot with the photographer of their choice, however, is not ethical. This is an area where agents often take great advantage of unsuspecting, aspiring actors. They'll charge you far above and beyond the going rate for the photographer and pocket much of the money themselves. It is a good idea, however, to get referrals to a few good, reasonably-priced photographers in your area. You can get rec-

ommendations from agents, the state film commission, or actors who've been around for a
while.

If the agents do not require you to do a scene
for them, and they've never seen your work
elsewhere, be cautious. Would you agree to be
a sales rep for a product you know nothing
about? Remember, it's one thing to get an
agent, and another to get an agent who believes
in you and can market you properly.

Some agents may tell you that you need more
experience, or need more training before they
can take you on as a client. This is fine, as
long as the phrase, . . ."so we'll just sign
you up in our classes, and then you'll get
plenty of work". . . doesn't follow. SAG-franchised agents are not allowed to teach classes for the obvious reason of possible conflict
of interest.

3. What clients/companies has your agency pro-vided talent for?

This answer will tell you how well-established
the agency is. Don't let the agent be vague.
Get specifics.

4. What training do your agents have?

This will give you an idea of the agents' ability to deal with industry issues.

5. If I join with you, can you guarantee me work?

An agent can *never* guarantee you work, since the agent is not in a position to do the actual hiring.

6. Are there actors working as employees in your agency?

Although there aren't supposed to be, actors are often hired to answer phones or do other odd jobs at an agency. It's rarely to your advantage. When acting jobs come in, these employees will most likely be 'looking out for #1.'

7. How many actors do they already represent that are in the same category as you?

If there are too many people like you in an agency, you are facing immediate competition. It's hard enough to make it without facing fierce competition from people in your own agency.

CHAPTER THREE

THE UNIONS

Please note that SAG and AFTRA rules and regulations change quite often. If you have any questions about rulings in your area, please refer to **www.actingacrossamerica.com** or Appendix D and call your regional union office for current information.

You've probably heard people talk about the unions in relation to actors, and you might be befuddled by what they are, who they are, and why they are. In this chapter, I'll answer some of those questions for you.

What are the actors' unions?

The union which covers all projects shot on film is the Screen Actors Guild, more commonly referred to as *SAG*. Video projects are covered by either SAG or the American Federation of Television and Radio Artists *(AFTRA)*. The stage union is Actors' Equity Association *(Equity or AEA)*. For the purposes of this book, I will be covering only SAG and AFTRA.

'Film' refers to 8mm, 16mm, 35mm, 70mm and several other large formats. Films are most commonly shot on 35mm film. Film for movie cameras is like the film which you use in your 35mm camera. Movie film needs to be developed just like film for still cameras and is also ruined by exposure to light before its use. When using film, the process of working with it is called 'filming' or 'shooting.'

'Taping' refers only to working with video, although working with video can also be called a *shoot*. Professional video cameras are in a digital or beta format, whereas your home video camera is VHS, 8mm, super 8, or digital. Like your home video camera, professional tape can be viewed as soon as something is taped on it, it can be used over, although it loses quality each time (unless it's digital).

You'll note, I said that video shoots can be covered by either SAG or AFTRA. The same is not true for film, which is only covered by

SAG. The medium in which the project is shot determines which union will be used, not the final viewing venue. In other words, a commercial which will only be shown on TV, but is shot on film, will be SAG. Movies of the Week *(MOWs)* which you watch on TV are also shot on film and therefore fall under the jurisdiction of SAG , not AFTRA. Voice work which will be used in a SAG or AFTRA project also comes under the jurisdiction of the unions, and all rules, regulations and payment schedules apply. Under most circumstances, regionally, extras are not under the jurisdiction of the unions, neither are stand-ins or photo doubles. As an actor you are paid the same, regardless of which union is used. Later in this chapter, I'll detail some of the other ways in which you will be affected if the project is either SAG or AFTRA.

Are projects automatically done through either SAG or AFTRA?

No.

No project is automatically done through any union. A company has to sign an intensive contract promising to adhere to all of the union rules in order to be able to use union actors. Once that company has signed a SAG or AFTRA contract, it has become a 'signator.'

Once a company becomes a signator to either SAG or AFTRA, all shows which they produce will be bound by that contract. Because most big production companies don't want to be bound by a contract for all future projects, they will usually create a separate company for each production. At that point, they choose whether or not to do the project through a SAG contract, an AFTRA contract or non-union.

Let's say that the *Smith/Jones Company* is a production company which is not a signator to any union. They are preparing to make a video documentary about trains. For this particular project, they will form a corporation named something like 'Tracks, Inc.', and *Tracks, Inc.* will become the signator to AFTRA. Any legal or union problems stemming from the railroad documentary will only affect *Tracks, Inc.*, and not *Smith/Jones Productions.*

Why are projects done through unions at all?

Throughout this book, when I refer to 'unions,' I specifically mean SAG or AFTRA. There are many, many other unions which apply to the film and television industry which do not affect actors' contracts. Some of those are the *DGA* (the Director's Guild of America), which oversees directors, assistant and associate directors and production managers; *WGA* (the Writer's Guild of America), which handles writers' contracts; and other *AFL-CIO* affiliated unions. Many projects which are union through SAG or AFTRA are not 'union' from any other standpoint.

Union contracts intrinsically carry with them situations which may complicate the paperwork to be done by the signators. People, therefore, wonder why a production would use SAG or AFTRA when the camera crew, drivers, and make-up people are non-union. The simple answer to that quandary is that a production company can not cast one acting union member and hire non-union members from there on out. In other words, if one actor in a project is union, they all have to be. Since most actors with name recognition are union members, the production company has to become a signator. You have to be in the union to work in a union film.

There are, luckily, exceptions to this, such as a film of a very specific genre which may not require name actors in order to get distribution. The genre itself is the selling point. For example, a martial arts film may be made with top-rank martial artists who are not members of SAG or AFTRA. In an IMAX film, the grandiose format of the film itself is the star.

On a non-union film, there is no real basis for negotiation. Many non-union films pay the same base rate as SAG or AFTRA, and sometimes more. There is no discrepancy in pay under a SAG or AFTRA contract, whether you're speaking one word or an entire Shakespearean monologue. This is not usually true of a non-union film, which tends to be negotiated on the basis of how large your role is. From an actor's standpoint, the biggest differences are that you will have no overtime or consecutive employment on a non-union shoot, and the production company will not have to make *P&W* (Pension and Welfare) contributions, or ever pay you residuals. Federal and state governments, of course, don't care whether the project is union or not. They take their share in taxes either way.

How do I get into a union?

You have to be a union member to be cast in a union project, but you have to work at least one union project before you can become a union member. It sounds like a giant Catch-22. How do you get around that?

There are three basic ways, and they all involve a *Taft-Hartley.*

Here's how it applies to SAG. (AFTRA doesn't use Taft-Hartleys, but the process is basically the same.) Although a SAG signator guarantees that it will make all best efforts to attempt to cast a role with a SAG member (this is called 'preference of employment'), there are occasions when an audition will open up for non-union members, or when a non-union member may be cast because of the right look, talent, accent—the possibilities are endless.

I've heard casting directors joke that SAG has refused so many Taft-Hartleys that you need to be casting a 6'8" albino basket weaver before they'll consent to the fact that perhaps you couldn't find that actor within the SAG membership. That example may be a little extreme, but specific talents do certainly help in getting a Taft-Hartley through. A person who can recite dialogue while jumping off a ramp on a Harley could probably be Taft-Hartleyed. So could an actor who is fluent in Swedish, Swahili and English, if those skills were required for the film.

Another allowance made by SAG is for recognizable groups. The Backstreet Boys or the Dallas Cowboys could be Taft-Hartleyed at no risk if the script called for them.

A non-union actor hired to be in a SAG film will need to have a Taft-Hartley completed by the casting director or producer. The Taft-Hartley will have a headshot and resume attached to it. As you can see on page 70, the information given by the production company needs to be quite precise. This form is never seen by the actor, and does not require her signature.

When SAG receives the Taft-Hartley, it is reviewed for its validity. The union then makes a decision as to whether or not the Taft-Hartley is accepted and if it is not accepted, the production company is fined for not giving preference of employment to a SAG member. It is understandable that any union with often 95% of its members unemployed would want a good reason to allow any new member to join. You now understand why a production company will be careful about hiring anyone who is not in the union. It certainly doesn't want to risk a fine.

The second way to become Taft-Hartleyed, besides having been cast off the bat, is often the more common way. You have been hired to work as an extra on a film. The scene is set in a coffee shop and involves you walking up to a table where the two stars of the movie are talking. You pour some coffee and walk away. After two rehearsals or camera run-throughs the director realizes that it is awkward for this waitress to approach the table without saying anything. He tells you (often to the producer's horror) to say, "Would you like more coffee?" before you actually pour it. And, bingo! You are now, for that day at least, treated like the other actors on the set.

Here's the avalanche effect that your five words of dialogue will have: The production company will need your headshot (or some picture) and resume, and will have to create a Taft-Hartley for you; the AD will need you to sign all of the appropriate SAG paperwork; you will be given a SAG contract for that day (which means that you'll have to fill out several forms, including a W-2 and I-9, so be prepared); the production company will need to retroactively *Station-12* you; you should get a dressing room; you will have an entry on the production report; you will be added to the call sheet; and your name will be added to the credits and cast list.

How does it affect you? Your salary just increased, possibly ten-fold. At lunch, you now eat with the talent instead of the extras, which means that you go to the front of the line; and the big one, if you're an aspiring actor, is that you have been Taft-Hartleyed, *which means that you can join the union.*

This scenario is called an *upgrade.* But remember that the upgrade only allows you to join the union if the film is being made under the jurisdiction of SAG. If the film is non-union, you are no closer to joining the union, but at least you got to say your first line in a movie!

I have seen situations too numerous to mention when an extra with absolutely no desire to act will be given lines on a set, while a bevy of extras are standing by who would give up their first-born child to be able to join SAG. They never said life was fair. If I am on the set, I will intervene in these situations, if possible, and make sure that an aspiring actor be given the lines. But I can't always be at the right place at the right time, as is shown in the next example.

Garrett van der Meer is a producer with whom I have had a strong working relationship, and that I happen to respect tremendously for his professionalism, concern for each crew member and, most impor-

SCREEN ACTORS GUILD   #15

TAFT/HARTLEY REPORT

ATTENTION: __Deborah Geter_____ATTACHED?:__XX_____RESUME*_____PHOTO

EMPLOYEE INFORMATION

NAME _____Clayton Taylor_____ SS#___528-89-3749_____
ADDRESS_____2388 West 90 South_____AGE (IF MINOR)___12____
CITY/STATE____Provo_____Ut_____ZIP__84601__PHONE(801) 377-1255__

EMPLOYER INFORMATION

NAME:_____Majestic Family Films I, LLC_____Check____AD AGENCY
One:____STUDIO
ADDRESS:____3487 W 2100 S_____ _X_PRODUCTION
COMPANY
CITY/STATE____Salt Lake City, UT ZIP_____84119____PHONE(801) 977-8260__

EMPLOYMENT INFORMATION

Check CONTRACT:_____DAILY   CATEGORY:___XX___ACTOR   OTHER _____
one: _____3-DAY   _____SINGER _____
        __XX_____WEEKLY   _____STUNT

WORK DATE (S)____March 3-6, 9,11, 1999_____SALARY __$1,620 /Wk_____

PRODUCTION TITLE_____A Dog's Tale_____PROD'N/COM'L _____

SHOOTING LOCATION (City & State)   SALT LAKE CITY, UTAH

REASON FOR HIRE (be specific)____After Auditioning numerous young actor's Clayton read the best and looked__
right for the part.

Employer is aware of General Provision, Section 14 of the Basic Agreement that applies to Theatrical and Television production, and Schedule B of Commercials Contract, wherein Preference of Employment shall be given to qualified professional actors (except as otherwise stated). Employer will pay to the Guild as liquidated damages, the sums indicated for each breach by the Employer of any provision of those sections.

SIGNATURE _Bryce Fillmore_____DATE___11/23/96____
         Producer or Casting director - indicate which

PRINT NAME__BRYCE FILLMORE - PRODUCER_____ PHONE(801) 977-8260__

*PLEASE BE CERTAIN RESUME LISTS ALL TRAINING AND/OR EXPERIENCE IN THE ENTERTAINMENT INDUSTRY.

tantly, his kindness and sense of humor. We were filming, under a SAG contract, *American Story,* a pilot for a show somewhat in the vein of *America's Most Wanted.* It was comprised of a series of reenactments of actual events. The budget was extremely tight—the kind of tight where any extra expenditure was felt.

We were shooting in a courthouse where our trial scene was underway. The courtroom was full of extras— people watching, as well as twelve jurors. The schedule had been grueling. We were tired. It was hectic, and Garrett asked me to go down the street and have a cup of coffee with him.

We weren't gone more than an hour - but that hour cost Garrett quite a bit more than two cups of coffee. It cost him over $10,000.00.

While we were gone, a foreign **AD** who was not familiar with SAG rules felt that the camera run-through of the jury did not feel right. He felt that it would work so much better if each jury member said either "guilty" or "not guilty" as we panned across each row of seats. Being the highest production authority on-set at the time, no one stopped him. By the time we returned, the scene had been shot. Wham! Twelve upgrades. Twelve SAG contracts. Twelve contributions to SAG pension and welfare.

And one very, very sorry AD.

Had the AD simply given the direction, but the scene had not yet been shot, we could have called a halt to the situation. However, once you've been directed by the director or the AD to say a specific word or line, and it has been shot, even if the camera wasn't on you, you are due an upgrade. It makes no difference if they say that the footage will not be used. They still owe you the upgrade and, hence, the ensuing payment.

Don't forget, The three keys to an upgrade are:

1. The dialogue was directed by the director or one of the ADs. (you can't take it upon yourself to speak in a scene if not told to do so.)

2. The direction was not generic to all of the extras present (i.e. twenty extras are standing in a room and the AD says, "When the star walks in, I want you all to say, 'Surprise!'"), but specific to you.

3. The scene was shot at least once, and you said the line (even if it was off-camera).

If you have an agent, and you are upgraded, call him as soon as you can get to a phone. Your agent is there so that there can be a good cop, bad cop relationship between you, your agent, and the production company. He can nicely call the production office and let the production coordinator know that you were recently upgraded and ask what can he do to help. Does the office need a headshot and resume? Of course they do, because they will have to send in a Taft-Hartley, but this is a nice way of saying, "We know about upgrades."

Most companies adhere willingly to their SAG signatory agreement, but there are always exceptions. DO NOT leave the set the day of your upgrade without having a contract in hand or, at least, without having signed some SAG paperwork, such as a time-sheet.

If you do not have an agent, make sure to let the 2nd AD know that you will need paperwork on the upgrade. Ask what information she will need from you to complete it. Again, do not leave the set without some documented proof of your upgrade, even if that means getting phone numbers from the extras working with you who could eventually serve as witnesses.

If the production company refuses to acknowledge the upgrade, don't let grass grow under your feet. Call your SAG regional office immediately (see **www.actingacrossamerica.com** and the Appendix), and have all of the pertinent information available: How you were originally hired; what was your date of employment; what is the name of the film, the name of production company; how did the upgrade occur? If for any reason, your regional office seems unresponsive, call the national office in LA. Remember, part of the signatory agreement which the production company signed states that they would acknowledge upgrades (per the SAG Codified Basic Agreement of 1977 Schedule A, Section 26). SAG has the option of closing the production down if they do not do so. That's a risk no producer wants to take.

The third way to get a Taft-Hartley is to do three UNION jobs as an extra. Retain your vouchers, and you will be able to join. Remember, though - there will be very few - if any - movies made in right-to-work states that will use union extras.

I have been Taft-Hartleyed! Now What?

You can join SAG at any time, but are not obligated to do so until you are cast in your next SAG project. However, until you have joined, you are still considered non-union and will not fall into the preference of employment SAG clause. This may cause you to miss out on auditions.

Once you have been Taft-Hartleyed and want to join SAG, call your local or regional office to find out how to do so. If there is an office within a relatively close distance, you may be asked to come in person to join. If there is not an office near you, arrangements will be made by mail. Even though SAG should have all of your pertinent records in their computers, bring any back-up material which you may have, specifically, a copy of the contract which you received when you had your speaking part. There are times when social security numbers are entered incorrectly, or any number of other things could have occurred to keep you from being shown in the computer. In order to avoid this, always check that your name and social security number are correct on any paperwork you sign.

Many regional offices go according to the national contract, which means that you will be paying over $1,000 to join SAG. Some regional offices have lesser fees to join in that area only. If you move to a national market, you will have to make up the difference. SAG will normally not assist you with a payment schedule.

There is a possibility that you may have to change your name in some way because someone else in SAG has exactly the same name that you do. That's where the 'J' came from in Michael J. Fox. Or, if you wish, you can change your name altogether, and take on a stage name for acting purposes. But that could confuse issues with the production accountant and your paycheck. If you don't have ID in your stage name, that paycheck could end up in a picture frame on your wall, because you can't cash it anywhere.

Once you have joined SAG, it will be your responsibility to make sure that SAG always has your most current address, phone number and agency representation so that they can properly assist you in tracking down talent payments and residuals, as well as having you listed in the agency division, which is how casting directors and producers find out who represents you.

Benefits of SAG membership are:

- Access to more acting work

- Good health insurance, once you've made $7,500 in a year (this amount includes residuals); great health insurance, once you've made $15,000

- A guarantee that you will be paid by the production company, since SAG requires a bond-protection of your safety and working conditions

- Extensive overtime payment

- Current information about the industry through newsletters, seminars, etc.

- Eligibility for AFTRA membership

Overall, SAG will act as a protector. Whereas many crew members end up never getting paid from an unreputable production company, the actor will, because SAG requires a bond from the production company before approving the participation of SAG members in a project. SAG also has clauses in its signatory agreement which protect the actor in regards to safety when it comes to pyrotechnics, animals, sets, etc. Nudity is also mentioned in the contract. Actors must be told before an audition of any required nudity or sexual situations in a film.

Detriments to joining SAG:

- You can no longer do any non-union acting work

- You will pay yearly dues which vary in proportion to your SAG income

How will producers and casting directors know that I'm a SAG member?

In a regional market, there are only a handful of legitimate casting directors. It probably would be a good idea to drop them a note, along with your headshot and resume, stating that you have joined SAG, and that you would like to be considered for any future SAG roles.

The bottom line for casting directors, confirming that you are, indeed, a SAG member in good standing (your dues are current) is a process called **Station 12.** (AFTRA simply calls this process 'cast clearance.')

Once a project has been cast, the casting director compiles a list which states the name of the actor, her social security number and start date, the day she is scheduled to begin filming. This list is either called in or faxed to Station 12, along with the name and address of the signator, casting director, location of hire and location of shoot. A list is faxed, called in, or mailed to the casting director giving one of four responses:

The following is an example of a station 12:

Screen Actors Guild - 5757 Wilshire Blvd., Los Angeles, CA 90036 - Station 12 (213) 549-6794

Fax # for Principals (213) 549-6792

STATION 12 INFORMATION FORM

DATE___5/20/98_____

CALLER #_____   PRODUCTION___The Long Road Home___
NAME *Majestic Family Films I, LLC.*   SIGNATORY *Ray Tremblay*_____
TEL.___*801-977-8260*___   EPISODE_____

ADDRESS *3487 West 2100 South*___   PRODUCTION CO___*Majestic family Films ,LLC*___
_*Salt Lake City, Utah 84119*___   PHONE__*801-977-8260*_____

LOCATION STATE___*Utah*_____   PRODUCTION TYPE _*Feature Film*_____

Social Security #	Name	Start Date	Catagory Codes	
	Michael Ansara	*6/01/98*		SAG
	Sandra Shotwell	*6/06/98*		SAG
	T. J. Lowther	*6/01/98*		SAG
	Al Harrington	*6/01/98*		SAG
	Billy DaMota	*6/09/98*		SAG
	Mary Elizabeth Winstead	*6/01/98*		T.H.
	Craig Clyde	*6/01/98*		SAG
	Joyce Cohen	*6/05/98*		SAG
	Kasey Clyde	*6/8/98*		T.H.

Explanation of Performer Category Codes

D - Dubbing	O - Other
E - Extra	P - Principle
G - Guest Star	R - Series Regular
L - Looping	S - Singer
N - Non-TH	V - Voice Over

1. **OK:** indicating that the actor is in good standing with SAG

2. **Station 12:** indicating that the actor can not work until she has cleared up a problem with SAG, usually non-payment of dues

3. **Must join:** the actor has been Taft-Hartleyed, but has not yet joined

4. **No record:** the actor must be Taft-Hartleyed

Only the *OK* response means that the production company is in the clear for using the actor. All other responses need to be dealt with before the actor works, or the production company will be fined.

I've heard horror stories about contracts. What do I need to watch for?

Before you receive an actual contract, your agency may be given a *deal memo.* The deal memo relates all of the conditions of the contract.

SAG contracts are a standard form, and as a SAG member you are not allowed to waive any portion of that contract without SAG's prior approval. There are also contracts negotiated on a *Favored Nations* basis. This means that no actor will receive more privileges than any other. It will hold true, not only for salaries, but for fringes, as well. I once saw an actor threaten to quit a film because the actor in the dressing room next to him had two mirrors, and he only had one.

There are three basic types of SAG contracts: Day player, three-day (TV only) or weekly player. A day player contract does not necessarily mean that you are only working for one day. If you are on a daily contract and work a second day, you will not fill out another contract. This is normal, as long as you are signing SAG time sheets on the set.

If you work over three days in one week, it will be less expensive for the production company to put you on a weekly contract. The basic difference between the daily and weekly is that the weekly rate is, of course, substantially less on a daily basis. You still get overtime with a weekly contract, and there are other minor considerations, such as the producers being allowed more time for wardrobe fittings. But, for the most part, the basic rules remain the same.

Here's the day player contract.

**THE PERFORMER MAY NOT WAIVE ANY PROVISION OF THIS CONTRACT
WITHOUT THE WRITTEN CONSENT OF SCREEN ACTORS GUILD, INC.**

**SCREEN ACTORS GUILD
DAILY CONTRACT
(DAY PERFORMER)
FOR THEATRICAL MOTION PICTURES**

Company__ Majestic Family Films I, LLC. Date__ 2/20/99 _____

Date Employment Starts____ March 1, 1999 ____ Performer Name_ Michelle Fillmore _____

Production Title__ A Dog's Tale _____ Address___ ████████████████ _____

Production Number_____ Telephone No.___████████████ _____

Role____ Emily _____ Social Security No.____ ████████ _____

Daily Rate $__ 466.00 _____ Legal Resident of (State)___ Utah _____

Weekly Conversion Rate $_____ Citizen of U.S.___ XX ____Yes_____No

Wardrobe supplied by Performer_____Yes_____No

If so, number of outfits_____ @ $_____

Complete for "Drop-And-Pick-Up" Deals ONLY:

Firm recall date on _____ or

on or after*_____

("On or after" recall only applies to pick-up as Weekly Performer)

As ☐ Day Performer   ☐ Weekly Performer

*Means date specified or within 24 hours thereafter

(formal)_____ @ $_____

Date of Performer's next engagement_____

The employment is subject to all of the provisions and conditions applicable to the employment of DAY PERFORMER contained or provided for in the Producer-Screen Actors Guild Codified Basic Agreement as the same may be supplemented and/or amended.

The Performer (does) (does not) hereby authorize the Producer to deduct from the compensation hereinabove specified an amount equal to _____ per cent of each installment of compensation due the Performer hereunder, and to pay the amount so deducted to the Motion Picture and Television Relief Fund of America, Inc.

Special Provisions:

PRODUCER_ Bryce Fillmore _____   PERFORMER_ *Terri Fillmore* _____
                                                         Michelle Fillmore
BY_ *Bryce Fillmore* _____

Production time reports are available on the set at the end of each day.
Such reports shall be signed or initialed by the Performer.

Attached hereto for your use is Declaration Regarding Income Tax Withholding.

NOTICE TO PERFORMER: IT IS IMPORTANT THAT YOU RETAIN A COPY OF THIS CONTRACT FOR YOUR PERMA-
                     NENT RECORDS.

ENTERPRISE STATIONERS, 7401 SUNSET BLVD., LOS ANGELES, CA 90046   (213) 876-3530   FAX (213) 876-4398   PRINTED ON NCR PAPER (NO CARBON REQUIRED)   **39**

80

Three-day contracts are only issued for television projects and are basically the same as the daily and weekly contracts.

Because the contracts are standard, there are only a few things which you need to watch for:

- Make sure that your name is spelled correctly.

- Check your address and phone number for mistakes.

- Check your social security number for mistakes.

The number of outfits which you have provided for the shoot needs to be filled-in so that your wardrobe allowance can be determined; although you may not want to fill it in until the end of the shoot. You are not paid for the number of outfits you bring, only for the ones which you wear. A change of hat or shoes does not constitute a wardrobe change. As you can see on the contract, there is a different rate for evening wear. Make sure that the correct items are checked off.

Check to see that the rate on the contract is what you agreed to. If your rate is *scale plus ten,* it may be stated as such, or the plus ten may be built into the stated rate (if scale is $500, and you agreed to scale plus ten, it may be listed as such, or as $550).

Drop/Pick-Up. If you are on a drop/pick-up, make sure that the box in the middle of the contract is filled in, as well as *Date of performer's next engagement.* (Drop/Pick-Ups will be covered in full in the section entitled: *What will affect my paycheck? p. 83*)

Don't leave the set without having a copy of your contract. When your contract is presented to you, it probably will not have the signature of the production company representative on it. It is still a binding contract. Although the contract must be given to you on the set, according to SAG rules, you are not obligated to sign it on the set. If you feel uncomfortable about any aspect of it, feel free to take it to your agent. It is, however, standard to sign it on the set but be sure that you have a copy to take with you.

Along with the contract, you will have to fill out two forms which need to be provided for any sort of employment in the United States: A **W-2** and an **I-9**. Do not ask the production staff how to fill these out. The forms have nothing to do with the production company. They are federal forms.

In order to fill out your W-2, you will need to know how many deductions you would like to claim. If you don't know what to claim, check with your accountant before coming out to the set. If you have incorporated yourself, you will not fill out a W-2, but will need your corporation's federal ID number for a separate form. In this case, you are called a *loan out;* i.e. the John Doe corporation is loaning out the services of John Doe.

The I-9 form is to prove that you can legally work in the United States. You will be required to furnish either a passport, or two forms of the following: Valid driver's license, military ID, state ID, social security card, and/or birth certificate. School IDs, library cards, etc., are not valid forms of identification for this purpose.

I recommend that you make copies of your driver's license and social security card so that you can hand them in with your I-9. If you are not a citizen of the U.S., and have a work permit, you will need to furnish a copy of it. If you are not a citizen of the U.S. and do not have the appropriate work permits, you will not be allowed to work. Remember, children need to fill out an I-9 as well, so get your children's social security cards and birth certificates together.

If you do not have the documents needed to fill out an I-9, they can be brought to the production office at a later date; but any procedure out of the norm is not only more work for you, it could keep you from getting your check on time.

Many agents require that your check be sent to their office so that you are obliged to pick up the check in person, and thus, pay your 10% on the spot. In order for this to happen, you will have to sign an authorization allowing the production accountant to release your check directly to your agent.

Another form which you may be asked to sign is a production company waiver. These do not compromise any SAG standards, and can consist of pages and pages of legal paragraphs. They are simply additional protection clauses for the production company. I have never seen one that was not okay to sign, but, again, if you are not comfortable with it, have your agent look at it before you do sign.

What Will affect my paycheck?

SAG and AFTRA have the same basic rates. SAG contracts are negotiated through different divisions; theatrical motion picture, television, commercial, industrial and interactive.

The base pay for both unions is called *scale.* This is the minimum amount that you can be paid while working on a SAG or AFTRA project. I will use the ficticious amount of $500 as the scale pay for the following example. If a film role is offered to you at scale, and your agent does not demand 'plus ten' or +10%, you can not, according to union rules, pay a commission to your agent, because, as stated earlier, YOU must make a *minimum* of $500.

Assuming that your agent has demanded plus ten, it will be built into your paycheck, and you will receive $550, minus taxes. Your agent gets 10% of your gross negotiated pay and overtime, but does not receive commissions on penalties, adjustments or wardrobe allowances. Agents who don't know better will take 10% off the top.

Be sure that doesn't happen. In the above example, your agent would get $50, not 10% of the amount paid to you ($55), which would actually be 11% of your gross. You may, at times, hear of someone negotiating a deal at double scale, which is exactly what it indicates. From that point on, the contract is negotiated in straight dollar amounts.

The same pay scale applies to an eight-hour day. If you are shooting in the same area where you were hired, you are on a *studio player rate.* If you were hired in one area, and traveled to a location, you are a *location player.* Those of you reading this book who are only interested in working regionally will almost always be hired on a studio basis. If you are a studio hire, your eight hours begin upon sign-in at the set and end upon sign-out. If you are a *location player,* your eight hours start when you are picked up from wherever you're staying, and end when you're dropped off.

Since filming days are rarely less than twelve hours, here's what your paycheck would look like during a thirteen-hour day as either a studio player or a location player.

studio player:

- **Arrive on set at 7:00 am**

- **7:00 am - 3:30 pm**
  (less half-hour for lunch), Base pay
  (8 hrs. x $62.50/hr.) $500.00

- **3:30 pm - 5:30 pm, Overtime**
  (2 hrs. @ 1.5 times regular pay) $187.50

- **5:30 pm - 8:00 pm**
  (less half-hour, second meal), golden time
  (2 hrs. @ double-time) $250.00

            Actor's Total Pay $937.50

| +10% agent's commission | $ 93.75 |
| + 2 wardrobe allowances | $ 30.00 |

- **Paycheck Gross** $1061.25

On top of this the production company makes Pension & Welfare contributions, as well as paying FICA, etc.

Location Hire:

- **6:00 am pick-up**

- **Arrive on set, 7:00 am**

- **Wrap, 8:00 pm**
  (13 hrs., less one hour for lunch and second meal)

- **9:00 pm drop-off**

Actor's Total Pay	$1125.00
+10% agent's commission	$112.50
+ 2 wardrobe allowances	$30.00
Paycheck Gross	$1267.50

Plus P&W, FICA, etc.

The location hire worked exactly the same amount of time as the studio hire, and at the same rate. The difference lies in the two hours of driving time which are calculated at time-and-a-half, creating an additional $187.50.

It would seem that you're a lot better off being a location hire than a studio player and you are, if it's only for a day. But it all evens out in the end if the studio player is on for a week or more. The studio actor's base weekly pay is calculated on 44 hours. The location actor's is based on 48 hours. So the local actor will go into overtime more quickly than the location actor.

While we're on the subject of location vs. studio actors, I want to give you a psychological boost for your next - *or perhaps your first* - audition as a regional actor. Let's say you are going to audition for the part of a cop who says, "Slow down," to a motorist—the two biggest words of your life.

You've heard jokes and clichés about nepotism in the film industry. That guy's terrible. Who is he? The director's nephew? Nepotism certainly exists, but is not as rampant as one may believe in the film business. One reason for this is that, relative or not, no producer wants an unnecessary fine from SAG because of a disapproved Taft-Hartley. The other is that every element of a film is a direct reflection on the producer and the director, and neither will purposely compromise quality. Actors aren't the only people who have the Catch-22 problem. So do set decorators, script supervisors, make-up artists, casting directors, etc. They have problems similar to the ones you face in joining the union, but they can be excluded from getting a job at all, even if the film is non-union.

When a production manager hires a crew member, that person is sent off to do her job. There is no one to baby-sit, and there is no room for mistakes. A *UPM* has to be able to make the assumption that between the time he hires a prop person and the time a specific prop is needed on the set, the prop has been found, rented or bought and is ready when it's needed. If that prop is not ready and available, and filming is held up because of it, the prop person will never be able to forget it. The only way a UPM or producer can avoid such a problem is to either hire someone he already knows and has worked with, or a person who has come very highly recommended. Under those circumstances, you can imagine how hard it is to break in as a crew member.

So, you're driving to your audition and are running your lines (or words) through your head. You probably will be interspersing your dialogue with demons from deep within, making destructive comments such as: "You think you have a chance against the producer's daughter? Look at Tori Spelling!" Or, "I know the director will hate my New England accent. She'll bring in some well-spoken friend from California." Well, throw this in those demons' faces and let it give you extra confidence at your audition: Someone in your area will get the part. *So why not you?*

It's a day player job, and you're on the set for twelve and a half hours. You're probably wondering why you would be there for twelve and a half hours to say, "Slow down!" Well, believe me, one measly day player is the AD's last concern while preparing the call sheet the night before. That's great for you, because it will almost certainly get you some overtime.

Let's say, for example, that the cop works in full sunlight. The weather report says that there will be no sun until the afternoon, so the AD schedules your shoot for around 3:00 pm and brings you in for wardrobe and make-up at 2:00 pm. The next morning, cast and crew show up at 6:00 am, and the day couldn't be more beautiful. In fact, the *DP* tells the director that the sun is perfect to shoot that scene with the cop - the one you're in. But you're not there. Not a good position for the AD to be in. So, instead of risking such a situation, the AD will usually bring day players in first thing, just in case. And after eight hours (minus lunch), you're the one who profits.

Here are the conditions of our hypothetical situation: The actor hired will be a day player, will have one line to say, will be paid scale +10 (which, for the sake of convenience, we'll make $800/day), will wear his own clothes in the scene, and will work twelve and a half hours. The actual shooting location is one hour from town.

These conditions are identical for you, the regional actor, and the LA location hire.

Let's figure out what each of these actors will cost the production company, starting with you, the local actor.

• **First 8 hours** (less half-hour meal):	**$800**
• **Hours 9 and 10** (at time and a half)	**$300**
• **Hours 11 and 12** (at double-time):	**$400**
Subtotal	**$1500**
• **Add approximately 40%** **in pension and welfare and** **other employer contributions:**	**$600**
• **Agent's commission:**	**$150**
• **Wardrobe allowance:**	**$30**
• **Paycheck Gross**	**$2265**

The producers will need to pay you almost $2300 to deliver one line. Now, let's add on the expenses of bringing an actor in from LA.

• **The base pay remains the same**	**$2265**

• **First-class airfare** (required), approximately	$1000
• **Two days first-class hotel** (travel and work day)	$ 300
• **Per diem for two travel days, one work day**	$ 150
• **Two travel days pay**	$1600
Subtotal	$5245
• **Pension & Welfare, Employer Contributions**	$ 640
• **Agent's commission on two travel days**	$ 160
Total	$6115

Here's the final point. When hired as a local actor, your work day starts when you get to the set, and ends when you leave the set. The out-of-town actor's pay starts when she is picked up at the hotel, and ends when she is dropped off at the hotel at the end of the work day.

Remember, we established that the set was one hour from town, which means that the out-of-town actor is working a 14-and-a-half-hour day, adding two hours of double time to her pay.

• **Two hours @ double time**	$400
• **Employer contribution**	$160
• **10% agent's commission**	$40
Grand Total	$7705

Now, go into that audition and kick some butt, because they're going to hire you, and you're going to save them a lot of money!

What other things on the set can affect your pay? On location, an actor has to be given a full sit-down, hot lunch within six hours of arriving on the set. (There are some very complex exceptions to this which need not be covered.) If that does not occur, the actor is given a meal penalty, which is paid in the following increments: The first half-hour is $25, the second half-hour is $35, and each half-hour after that is $50 until you are finally fed. These meal penalties are documented through the SAG paperwork that you initial on the set. Keep in mind that the initialing of SAG paperwork on the set does not mean that you approve of the information. If you have a problem with the hours that were listed for your set call, make-up, meal breaks, or release, you can still take it up with your agent or directly with the union.

A situation may arise which the stunt coordinator feels is a bit unsafe for you, such as having to run down a street while it is wet. It's something that you do all the time, and you have no qualms about it, but let the experts on the set do their work. It may be suggested that a stunt person double you during the running up to the car, at which time you are inserted, saying your infamous, "Slow down!" Or you may be asked if you're comfortable doing it, and then given a stunt adjustment, more commonly known on the set as a 'bump.' No bump is worth its money if you have any fear of doing what is being asked of you. Nancy Reagan would encourage you to "Just Say No," and so would I.

If you are given a call time, and drive to the set, you will be paid for a full day's work at the scale rate, whether you work two hours, two minutes, or are sent home immediately.

What happens if you are called in to work on Monday? They briefly show you running up the street, but never get to your dialogue. You're called back on Tuesday, and you never even get into wardrobe. On Wednesday, they realize that they just won't be able to get to you, so they give you a day off altogether. On Thursday, they call you in and you finally shoot your scene. How will you be paid?

When you don't have dialogue, you're an extra, right? That would be Monday. Same for Tuesday. When you have a day off, you're not paid, right? So you finally get your SAG pay on Thursday. WRONG!

When you are hired as an actor from the start, you can not work on that particular film in any other capacity. You are an actor. So on

Monday and Tuesday, you've made full SAG pay during your time on the set. And on Wednesday, you have, too. This is due to the *consecutive employment* clause of the SAG contract.

As a day player, you can not be given a day off, and then brought back to work. You will be paid your full rate for the day off. Then, on Thursday, you finally come to the set and do your work. In order to say two words, you will be paid for four full days at SAG scale. It will, however, be noted on the production report that on Tuesday and Wednesday, you were paid, but not filmed, and those two days of pay will be exempt when it comes to residual payments.

I was the regional casting director on a movie of the week entitled *Standoff at Marion* about a fundamentalist Mormon family that ended up being involved in the longest FBI standoff until Waco. The movie starred Dennis Franz, Ed Begley, Jr., and Rex Linn. It was a tough mountain shoot in the dead of winter.

The story included dozens of police officers and SWAT team members, and since it was a standoff, we saw the same faces over and over again. A talented local actor by the name of Craig Clyde had four days of employment during the shoot; and yet, because of the way his days were scheduled (the grid made up by the AD to show the days when actors work is called a *day out of days*), he was paid for every single day of the shoot.

Craig has directed several movies, such as *A Christmas Tale, Little Heroes* and *Legend of Wolf Mountain,* but I doubt that he'll forget his experiences on *Standoff at Marion!* I guess the perfect job for a local actor is to also be the one who makes up the schedule!

SAG does have several exceptions to the consecutive employment clause, the most common one being known as a *drop/pick-up.*

Craig Clyde

Here's an actual day out of days:

March	Day of Month:	1	2	3	4	5	6	7	8	9	10	11	12	Rehearse	Travel	Work	Hold	Holiday	Loop
	Day Of Week:	M	Tu	W	Th	F	Sa	Su	M	Tu	W	Th	F						
	Shooting Days:	1	2	3	4	5	6		7	8	9	10	11						
1. Professor									SW	W	W	WF				4			
2. Tim			SW	W	W	W		H	W	H	WF					6	2		
3. Haley			SW	W	H	W		W	W	WF						6	1		
4. Mary (Tim's Mother)				SW	W	WF										3			
5. Henry (Tim's Father)			SW	W	W	WF			I							4			
6. Deputy Davidson			SW	H	H	H		H	W	W	H	WF				4	5		
7. Keith "The Bully" Carmody			SWF						I							1			
8. Owen Slade												SWF				1			
9. Mr. Clotfelter									SW	WF						2			
10. Harold	SW															1			
11. Emily	SW															1			
12. Annabelle			SWF													1			
13. Nat the Nordic Bully			SWF													1			
20. Tim the Dog	SW	W	W	W	W	W		W	W	W	H	WF				10	1		
21. Karen the Dog				SW	H	H		H	W	W	H	WF				3	5		

Report created Sun, Dec 26, 1999 — Page 1

Production companies are allowed one drop/pick-up per actor, per project. A drop/pick-up, as the name indicates, means that the production company can drop the actor and pick him up again later. This can only occur when there are ten working days between the drop and the pick up.

The drop/pick-up is shown on your contract. Go back to page 80 and you will see on the SAG daily contract that there is a drop/pick-up box in the left center of the page. If the company is picking you up as a day player, they have to give the specific date on which it will happen. If they don't work you on that day, they will still need to pay you from that pick-up date through the day that you actually work. When picking you up as a weekly, the production company has a twenty-four-hour leeway called an *on or about* date. Either way, the pick-up date needs to be indicated not only in the box, but on the line to the right of it as well, which reads, "Date of performer's next engagement."

Consecutive employment is also not required between such situations as a rehearsal (for which you are paid in full) and your regular employment on the set. Nor is it required in the case of a reshoot due to any number of problems, or a rewrite which creates more filming of your character.

SAG has a contract which is referred to as either the SAG modified low-budget agreement, the modified agreement, or the low-budget agreement. This contract is granted to production companies who can prove that their budget will be below $2 million. The low budget agreement doesn't affect the actor as much from the scale as it does other conditions, such as the removal of the consecutive employment clause.

When shooting for more than one day, you may run into a ***turn around*** problem. The SAG contract guarantees actors that they will get twelve hours off from one day of shooting to the next, and a thirty-six-hour rest once a week. If the production company brings you back before you have received the full rest period, it is referred to as a *forced call.* Being in turnaround violation is excruciatingly expensive for the production companies, as it actually takes you into an additional day of pay.

If you are asked to come to an audition memorized (or ***off-book***), it ceases to be an ***audition,*** and becomes a ***screentest.*** And when you go to a screentest and don't get the part, the production company must pay you a half day's pay. I personally will not allow actors to come into my auditions without their sides in hand for two reasons— one: It's not allowable according to the SAG contract and two: No matter how memorized you think you are, there's a good chance that you'll lose your train of thought when facing the casting director.

You may be entitled to other peripheral payments as well. You can only be kept at an audition for one hour, from the time your audition was scheduled until the time you sign out. If you are kept for a longer period, you will be paid on a pro-rated amount. If, however, you were more than five minutes late, the production company's obligation to release you within one hour is waived.

The production company is allowed a specific amount of time with you for wardrobe fittings. The time period and rate changes periodically. This is something that your agent should stay on top of.

If a production company requires you to drive what you feel is an extensive distance, you may also be entitled to drive-to money. Check at your local SAG office to see what your area's zone is.

The production company must pay its talent within ten business days.

Residuals are like pennies from heaven! They come when you least expect them and often when they're most needed. Residual checks are payments to the actors on sales made by the owners of a project in which you were cast. The formula used to calculate residuals was certainly created by a very vindictive ex-IRS agent. It takes a rocket scientist to figure it out. If you want the formula, feel free to call your SAG office, because I'm not going to attempt to cover it here. Your first residual checks on a project will be for the largest amount of money. The dollar amount will decrease from then on, until it dwindles away to almost nothing.

Suffice it to say, you will quickly learn to recognize that windowed envelope with the SAG logo on it. Opening it is somewhat akin to scratching off the glitter on lottery tickets. You can score big time or end up with a check for less than the cost of the stamp it took to mail the envelope.

An actor by the name of James Cash was hired as Henry Fonda's photo double during the filming of *On Golden Pond* because of his uncanny resemblance to the late actor. Although Jim was only in his thirties at the time, when he was made up, Jane Fonda actually had to look twice to see which one was her dad. It was a great job in a beautiful setting, and Jim was put on a SAG contract to boot, even though the production company was under no obligation to do so for a photo double.

One week into the shoot, the crippling SAG strike of 1980 hit. It completely closed down the industry. Films couldn't be made without actors. *On Golden Pond* very quickly got a 'sweetheart agreement' from SAG, which meant that the producers agreed to retroactively pay the actors whatever the outcome of the strike would require. This was granted due to the age of the actors and the delicate condition of Henry Fonda. Thank God it was. Henry Fonda received the Academy Award for Best Actor the following year and died shortly thereafter.

The shutdown, albeit temporary, had a negative financial impact on the film, and Jim Cash was taken off the SAG contract and worked the rest of the film for a low day rate. Jim's total SAG pay, which is what his residuals would be based on, was well below $1,000.

Approximately one year later, Jim went to the mailbox of his tiny studio apartment in LA and opened the residual envelope to find a check for over $16,000. Within a couple of years, he had made an additional $30,000.

Hold on! Don't put the book down and run out to find an agent quite yet. I still have more to tell you.

SAG and AFTRA were created for very legitimate reasons. Actors needed protection. They worked long hours with inadequate compensation, consideration or safety. When the federal child labor laws were enacted, they specifically excluded performers!

Today, SAG and AFTRA still do many wonderful things to protect their members, but because so many of the rules are gray, you can get one interpretation from one SAG office and a totally different one from another. It's rare to call a regional office and get an instant answer at all. They almost always have to check into it and get back to you.

My advice to you is to use logic in your dealings with SAG. And know the rules! If you've paid attention during this chapter on SAG and AFTRA, you're now well on your way to doing just that.

Jan Felt's break!

I was casting a MOW entitled Siege at Alta View, starring Teri Garr and Harry Hamlin. Jan was having a hard time getting into any auditions other than small local commercials with other local casting directors, because her resume consisted only of church plays.

Although I've sometimes regretted it, I pride myself on being open to seeing anyone who's right for the part. Jan came in and read and absolutely knocked my socks off! Fortunately, she did the same for the director, who cast her in a co-starring role!

Of all the actors I've worked with, Jan is one of the very, very few who is an absolute natural. I am a big fan.

Right-To-Work States

Now, forget everything I've told you, because we're now going to talk about *right-to-work* states!

The crux of *right-to-work* is that no individual may be discriminated against for not belonging to a union. Twenty-one states (see **www.actingacrossamerica.com** and the Appendix) are right-to-work. Many of the SAG and AFTRA rules which I just told you about are not enforceable in right-to-work states.

In the case of an actor being Taft-Hartleyed in a right-to-work state, the casting director or producer will need to complete all of the same paperwork, but the Taft-Hartley can not be denied by SAG. This last point will be argued, not only by SAG, but by many regional casting directors and producers who have been fined by SAG and have paid the fine for denied Taft-Hartleys.

In the early 1980's, I did the regional casting on a movie of the week entitled *Incident at Dark River,* starring Mike Farrell and Tess Harper and produced by Mike's company, Farrell/Minoff Productions. The film was shot in a right-to-work state, and I Taft-Hartleyed numerous day and weekly players. The SAG office chose to fine Farrell/Minoff Productions for some of its Taft-Hartleys.

Farrell/Minoff Productions' legal counsel, Jim Leonard, consulted me on the issue, and after reviewing all SAG signatory contracts and the fact that we were hiring and shooting in a right-to-work state, I stood my ground in asserting that SAG had no right to enforce such a fine.

When SAG received a letter from Jim Leonard explaining why the fines were not legitimate, they dropped the fines. Mike Farrell is a SAG member himself, and *I have never tried to go around SAG rules.* I know the rules well, and I knew that the company which hired me was a signatory. I follow the rules so closely that I have, several times, had my casting job jeopardized by refusing to do something for a producer which is not allowed by SAG. But I will not go above and beyond what I am legally obligated to do.

Some rules and regulations don't change, however, such as the above example about Taft-Hartleys in right-to-work states. Another thing that doesn't change, but that few regional employers know, is that an actor only needs to be Taft-Hartleyed only once. The purpose of the Taft-Hartley is to enter the actor's Social Security number into SAG's computers so that there is a record of her employment. In right-to-work states where actors don't need to join the union after their first SAG employment, casting directors often run across people who've been Taft-Hartleyed and are now working again without having joined the union.

Regional SAG offices will often tell the casting director that the actor needs to be Taft-Hartleyed again, causing the casting director a substantial amount of additional work in a job which already involves a lot of paperwork. Remember, for all of the reasons which I've given, it will be much easier for you to be Taft-Hartleyed in a right-to-work state.

How does the station 12 process work in a right-to-work state?

The initial process is exactly the same, and the casting director still receives the same printed-out responses: OK, Station-12, Must Join or No Record. But all responses other than No Record are crossed out, and read 'OK' instead. The casting director, as stated above, still needs to do the appropriate Taft-Hartley paperwork on a No Record.

If I join the union in a right-to-work state, can I still do non-union work?

No. However, as a SAG member, you can write to SAG and tell them that that are going to be 'Financial Core.' This means that you are dropping your rights to vote in SAG elections or hold office in SAG. You are still considered to be a SAG member, but you can now do non-union work.

But if almost all movies are SAG, what difference does it make that I can't do non-union work?

Most movies are SAG. But regional actors have far more venues in which to pursue their craft than just movies. Many infomercials, industrial films, CD-ROM projects and commercials are non-union. By joining the union, you are eliminating all of these sources of employment, although many actors will risk it anyway and work *off their card* on a non-union shoot.

What happens if SAG or AFTRA find out?

The actor is fined, and his membership may be revoked.

If I can no longer do non-union work after I join SAG and/or AFTRA, and yet I don't need to be a union member to get a union role in a right-to-work state, what's the point of joining?

Read on.

There are four assets to joining SAG or AFTRA:

1. You can put on your resume that you are a union member. It will give you more of an appearance of professionalism.

2. Many casting directors don't understand the implications of a right-to-work state. They still enforce the preference of employment clause, which eliminates non-union actors from preliminary auditions.

3. If you join SAG or AFTRA regionally, you are prepared to work in LA or New York if you choose to do so.

4. **Pay heed to this one:** When working on a SAG film, you get overtime, protection, and guarantee of payment because of SAG.. If gaining these assets, is it not ethically and morally right to join?

If I earn the minimum to get health insurance, wouldn't it be a good idea to join then?

If you earn the necessary minimum from a SAG signatory, you are entitled to your insurance *whether you join the union or not*. The insurance is not a gift from SAG. Every union production company you worked for paid into a fund, and the money was put into your name. Also, if the company is a SAG signatory, all overtime, penalties, meal penalties, drop/pick-ups, etc. are still applicable in a right-to-work state. The changes really only apply to issues affecting membership in the unions.

In a perfect world, a board would be formed in every right-to-work state which has a fair number of productions. That board would consist of a SAG and AFTRA representative, legal counsel, a representative of the state's employment division, actors, and most especially, signators, and they would meet monthly to clarify any new regulations and to see how those regulations apply in a right-to-work state. Until that happens, there will continue to be too much gray area for anyone's good, and the members of SAG and AFTRA will be the first to suffer.

CHAPTER FOUR
LOCATION SHOOTING VS. STUDIO SHOOTING

It's starting to look interesting. Now, you realistically ask yourself, I live in Austin, Texas (or Alexandria, Virginia, or Billings, Montana or. . .), what is there for me if I do decide to become an actor?

Obviously, not every single part of the United States has a lot of acting work, but every part has *some*. There is always a need for regional or local commercials, infomercials, industrials and voice-overs. Many of these projects are non-union, which means that you will have to start from scratch in negotiating your deal. There will be no guarantees or precedents set by the unions. There is usually little or no room for negotiation on such projects. The producers set their talent budget and stick to it. The philosophy is that if you're offered the part and don't want to do it for their rate, there are ten people standing behind you who do.

A regional or local project could pay anywhere from $100 per day (sometimes less) on up. The biggest negotiating point on such a project, however, is not the initial pay, but the pay for future runs. For example, a company makes a commercial which it then airs every single spring for the next ten years. We've all seen those commercials that just won't go away.

If you acted in such a commercial and were paid for a buyout, then you would see no additional pay when the commercial airs. If, however, your pay was negotiated on a certain run, you would be paid an agreed-upon amount for any future run.

Let's say that you're paid $1,000 for one day's work and a six week run of the commercial. You would, at the initial negotiations, decide how much you'll be paid for future runs. That could be 100% of the original, 80%, or anything else you negotiate.

When such projects are union, the residual pay is pre-negotiated for you.

Only big stars with a lot of clout get a percentage of the income generated by a project. The percentage which they receive is called *points.* I hope that each of you reading this book gets points one day!

When national projects, such as commercials, movies of the week or films come to your area, you will probably hear about them through you agent, the media or by word-of-mouth. Remember, your state's film commission has information on every one of those projects.

Why do studios and independent production companies leave LA to film?

For many, many reasons: The look that's needed for the shoot, the season (try shooting a wintry mountain scene right in LA), for accuracy (say, the movie is based in St. Louis), and sometimes for economics.

You already know that right-to-work states don't require the use of union labor. Many of these states, such as Texas, Florida, Utah and North Carolina, have become hotbeds for production for that reason. And, in turn, because a lot of projects shoot in those states, they tend to have a strong support system as far as crew, talent and equipment. Many states also give film companies attractive tax breaks. The U.S. is also losing a lot of productions to Canada, where production companies receive tremendous financial incentives such as hefty tax rebates.

Do they actually hire people on location?

The answer to that question depends on the budget. The bigger the budget, the fewer people they hire on location, since they can afford to hire, transport and lodge the people they are used to working with. This holds true for both actors and crew. But since many films are made on location to save money, many people are hired.

Let's use the example of a movie of the week which may have a budget of $2.8 million. In the realm of film making, this is a low budget. The lead three to six actors will be cast out of LA or New York by the principal casting director, and the local casting director will cast the remaining roles, usually about 20. These roles vary from a couple of days' work to simple one-liners. Since all local roles, in this case, would be paid scale, it wouldn't really matter if you had just a small part for one day. It would still pay well. And if you're not in the union yet, you would be Taft-Hartleyed.

So much of getting the part is your attitude. Attitude that you can do it, want to do it and will do it well. If you walk in with the attitude written all over your face and body language that says 'I know you're going to hire your sister from LA anyway, so why are you seeing me at all?' I guarantee you will not get the role. In order to give regional actors a psychological boost, I ask you to go back to Chapter 3 and see how much money the producer will save by casting a local actor.

The financial implications are great news for the regional actor and not necessarily bad news for the LA actor, either. First of all, remember that the starring and co-starring roles will come from LA, which gives an actor there the opportunity for a much meatier part. I also recommend, if you're an LA actor willing to put in a little extra effort, that you market yourself regionally. Make a list of the states where you have a grandma, a college roommate, a cousin. If you have a free place to stay in many towns around the country, and you're willing to fly or drive yourself to the location, you can try to get a role slated as local hire. Technically, if a casting director reads you in LA and you end up working on location, you are not considered a local hire, and all location expenses apply. Again, technically, to truly be a local hire, you must be auditioned by the local casting director. The bottom line, however, is the address that goes on your paperwork which you turn into the production company. If the address is a local address, you are, ultimately, a local hire. The logistics on this can be tricky as far as expenses and timing, but could be well worth your while financially.

Although many, many films are shot in LA and New York, the trend is to shoot on location to get a specific look, instead of trying to recreate it on a studio backlot. I don't see any sign of this trend dwindling, which gives all of you regional actors great promise for the future.

CHAPTER FIVE

THE SCAMS

It is never easier to prey on someone than when the subject at hand is a personal, or even easier, an emotional one.

Do you remember the movie *Paper Moon?* In that movie, Ryan O'Neal and a then very young Tatum O'Neal (who won an Oscar for the role) played a father and daughter who ran a very fruitful scam. They would read the obituaries daily, and go to the homes of the widows, where they would ask for the husband. The wife would, of course, tearfully tell the pair that he had just passed away. After expressing their condolences, they would tell the widow what a shame it was that he would never get to see the Bible he'd ordered for the family. Wracked with emotion, the widow would buy the Bible. A great scam. Almost as good as some of the scams I've seen pulled on actors.

I was once in the process of casting two projects simultaneously: A Disney series, and a pilot. Someone pointed out to me that the local newspaper where I was casting had an ad for a talent agency which was also 'casting' these two projects. I took the ad into the producer of the pilot, who called the agency on a speakerphone. The person on the other end confirmed to the unidentified caller that, for a fee of $50, he would be put on the casting tape for the two above-mentioned projects. When the producer revealed himself, the scam artist back-peddled, saying that he had been trying to reach me (he hadn't) to show me the tapes. The following day, the attorney general closed him down. Two things to remember here: Talent agents don't cast (actually, sometimes they do, but it is highly unethical) and, most importantly: NEVER, ever, under any circumstance, pay to audition!

Other things to watch out for are: Never pay to join a talent agency (extras agencies are exceptions), and watch out for ads in newspapers. If the agency is strong and well-established, it certainly will not be needing to advertise for talent. It will, on the contrary, be screening talent, and taking only a small percentage of those who apply.

I've covered this already, but stay away from agencies that force you to use their photographer, or require you to take their expensive acting classes before they take you on as talent. *They are absolutely correct to say you should be studying*, and they may also be correct in saying that you are not yet ready to go out on auditions because of your lack of training. If that is the case, look into other agencies to see what reaction you get. Then, find out what classes are worth the taking.

Nudity

Any film which requires nudity will disclose that information to the agent. I have cast many films which required nudity for various reasons. When that has been the case, the agents knew before the audition, and the people auditioning knew as well.

When auditioning for such roles, actors may or may not be asked to partially disrobe at the audition. If you go to an audition which had no mention of nudity, and the casting director asks you to disrobe, I would highly recommend not doing so. The decision is obviously yours, but use your head.

Legitimacy

Be careful of people who approach you on the street. Business cards can be printed up for almost nothing and anyone can create an identity for himself. With that warning in mind, I will also say that I have personally recruited many people from public places for auditions, especially children. You can imagine how sensitive an issue this is in these days of abductions and senseless crimes.

When I do this, I never approach the child first. I always approach the adult, and give them a full background on the project with which I'm involved. I then give them the phone number of the production company for which I'm working, and, if on location, the number of the local film commission. I ask them to please call those numbers to confirm my legitimacy and then call my office if they are indeed interested.

If a stranger approaches you or your child in any other manner, be very, very careful. Again, this is a deeply emotional scam. What parent doesn't think that their child is cute enough, or funny enough to be in front of the camera?

As I mentioned in an earlier chapter, look into new, hot things carefully before spending any money or involving precious children.

This may looK liKe a scam, but it's not.

Now, on the other hand, there are many things which might be construed as shady, but actually aren't. Let me profile some of these situations.

When on location, a production company will usually set up offices in the hotel where the crew is staying. Do not be alarmed if you are asked to come to an audition in a hotel. When you get there, if the circumstances don't seem right, there may be room for concern. You should see a sign-in table and at least one assistant. There should also be other actors in sight who are waiting to audition.

You may hear that Universal Studios is in town making a movie, and you decide to audition for it! Don't be concerned when you see 'XYZ Productions' or just the name of the film and no sign of

Universal. Universal may be behind the film, but there is actually a separate production company under contract to produce the film.

There may be situations at an audition when you are asked to use sides from a movie script which has nothing to do with the one at hand. Don't be alarmed. It happens. The real script may be in the middle of a huge rewrite; your character may have just been added; there are no sides yet. Again, the possibilities are endless. Don't let it concern you. You have an opportunity to do your thing for the casting director - go for it!

Another thing which is often touchy for the parents of a child who is auditioning is that the parent will rarely be allowed into the audition. When I'm auditioning children, I don't allow the parents in the room; but I do always have an assistant in the room with me. Not everyone does this, so it will have to be left to your discretion.

In fact, it is important that you take every step of your career with your heart and your eyes wide open. Be open and willing, but listen to your gut. Do what's right for you.

Part II:
The AUDITION

CHAPTER SIX
DEMYSTIFYING THE CASTING PROCESS

The six stages of an acting career are:
Who's Jane Doe?
Get me Jane Doe.
Jane Doe's too expensive.
Get me a Jane Doe type.
Get me a young Jane Doe.
Who's Jane Doe?

The unknown causes more anxiety than anything else. Part of an actor's fear of auditioning is just that: He doesn't know how the casting process works, he doesn't know the casting director, he's not familiar with the auditioning space. Let me address these issues and hopefully remove a layer of fear at your next reading.

Casting directors have to get their jobs just like anyone else. Sometimes a casting director does all of the casting for a certain company. A casting director usually has directors and producers that he's close to that hire him for all of their projects. But most of the time, the casting director has to come in for a job interview just like anyone else.

Once we get the job, not only are we doing the best job possible on the film at hand, but we are also hoping to develop an ongoing working relationship with the people who hired us.

What does a 'good job' mean for a casting director? It means putting together a talented, professional cast, on time and on-budget, while keeping a strong balance between the director and the producer. A casting director can assemble a cast of thirty wonderful actors and never once hear, "Atta boy!" But watch what happens when a casting director happens to cast someone who is a troublemaker on the set ,has a drinking problem, any number of things. It ends up being a reflection on the casting director. At auditions, besides talent, we are looking for any signs which could mean trouble in the future.

Once a casting director is hired, he receives a script and does a breakdown. This means that he makes a list of all the characters, and writes a brief description of each. In order to get funding for a project, producers often have to have a star attached to the project, which means that the casting director may or may not be casting the actual lead(s). The casting director's pay begins at this time, as does a whole lot of work—work that has nothing to do with reading actors.

If the casting is being done in LA, the casting director sends the breakdown out to the Breakdown Services, a company which faxes breakdowns to all of the agents who are members. Breakdown Services is a company which often has a project's breakdown out to agents within an hour after receiving it. Some breakdowns come across the Internet as well.

You'll find that agents usually don't like taking phone calls first thing in the morning, because that's the time they spend pursuing the break-downs and pulling the talent which they feel is best-suited for a par-ticular role. In other words, they've seen on a breakdown that there is a role for a 28-year-old Asian woman who rides horses well. You are actually a 31-year-old Asian woman, but look younger, and have ridden all your life. It's a good match. So the agent takes one of your headshots and resumes from the file and submits it to the casting director, along with any other suitable match from that agency. These submissions are often hand-delivered by a messenger, rather than waiting for the mail system to get them to the casting director.

The casting director reviews the submissions and calls the agent back to give him the names and times at which they want to see particular people. I stress **times** because casting directors, at an initial audition, may be seeing people as closely together as every five minutes. That's why you get times like 10:55 for your audition. Try to stick to that time if at all possible. Casting directors have an order in which they see people, and the schedules are tight.

Switching times can be a big inconvenience.

If the casting is being done regionally, the casting director will either distribute the breakdown to each agent, will have a cattle call adver-tised through the media, or, if he's familiar with the talent in that town, may just send in a list of the people he wants to see. From that point on, the auditions in LA or regionally are pretty much the same.

I am now going to tell you two things which may be the most important tips you will ever get. Pay heed, and you will do much, much better at auditions.

1. Keep in mind that casting directors are *people*. There are as many personalities as there are casting directors. If you luck into an audition with a warm, encouraging casting director that you truly feel is on your side, good for you. Use that positive energy and shine! But, sad to say, that attitude may be the exception.

    There's not enough room in this book for me to list why you may get a chilly reception from a casting director: He's seen 120 people today and is exhausted; he just got a phone call from the producer who is upset at the amount of the phone bill he just turned in; he's a frustrated actor and would rather be in your shoes; his son just broke his leg, and he'd rather be with him, and so on, and so on, and so on.

    All of these are reasons why you may feel completely shut out by the casting director. You may feel he hates you, that you don't stand a chance. Take a close look at the possible reasons for coldness which I listed. How many of them have anything to do with you? NONE. Yet 99% of the time, an actor will be prepared in the waiting area and feeling extremely confident, until she walks through the door and feels the chill. Don't let the casting director's attitude throw you. Walk in with dignity, give it your best, and leave with dignity. Being able to retain your presence will make a marked impression on the person who's reading you.

Remember, when you go to an audition, you're not on a date. You don't need to click with the casting person. You need to convey your talent. Do just that!

2. This point goes right along with the first one, but you'll probably think I'm out of my mind simply because it seems so backwards. When you walk into the casting space, act as though *you are the host and the person, or people, auditioning you are your guests*. It should be the other way around, right? It's their space. They have the control. Try this:

Gather a group of actors together and split them into two groups. Half are casting directors and half are actors waiting to audition. As casting people, you will realize that it is extremely tense bringing people in to audition. The more the actor puts the casting person at ease, the better the audition.

After days of initial auditions, the casting director will know who will and will not get a callback, or a second audition. Callbacks usually have the director in attendance, but a casting person may want to see you one more time alone before having you meet the director. The agents are called and told which of their people will have a callback. They may or may not be given a callback time at that point. Callbacks can be held the same day, or sometimes as much as a month later. Headshots and resumes of those not brought in for a callback are discarded.

What makes someone get or not get a callback? When you do get a callback, it's because something worked: The look was right, the read was good, you seemed capable of playing the part, and you did not seem like you'd be an embarrassment to the casting director (i.e., you weren't drunk, stoned, late, you didn't have an attitude, etc.). Any of the above reasons could also, in reverse, be why you didn't get an audition.

There could be one callback, there may be several. At the end of each callback, more people are eliminated. The director and casting director have discussions, and choices start to be made. It's then time to call the agents and let them know who's been cast. Once we've decided we want you, it's time to see whether or not we come to an agreement on the rate, and whether or not you're available to shoot on the days which we have scheduled. When that's settled, the casting process, on your end, is complete.

CHAPTER SEVEN
PREPARING TO GO TO AN AUDITION

Oh, boy! All of the preparation, money and hard work have paid off. You have an audition!

In this chapter, I deal specifically with what you can do to prepare for the audition before you ever get there.

When your agent calls to tell you about the audition, get as much information as you can and make sure the information is clear. Agents often call hundreds of people, and you may be one of many. It's an acting job that's at stake. Here's a checklist of what you need to know.

- **Where is the audition?** Be specific. Is there a suite number? If you are not sure where it is, look it up on a map. Or, better yet, drive by.

- **What time is the audition?** Think. How long will it take you to get there? Add twenty minutes to that for good measure.

- **Where are you supposed to park?** Union regulations state that free parking must be provided to actors when auditioning.

- **Who is the casting director?** Find out as much as you can about her. Have you auditioned for her before? What has she cast besides this? Did she say that she's looking for anything in particular?

- **Who is the casting assistant? Do you know him?**

- **Who are the production company, director and producer?**

- **What is the role? Name of character? Description of character?**

- **Is there nudity/violence, etc.?**

- **Will the audition be on-camera?**

- **Are the sides available in advance?**

Your agent may not have in-depth answers to the above questions, but get as much as you can, and once you have that, do some homework of your own. According to SAG rules, your agent should have a copy of the script available in his office. If there are sides available before the audition, get them as soon as possible. In Los Angeles, you can get them quickly from Shofax., Castnet, or Sides Express. The more time you have to prepare, the better.

Check your appointment book, and make sure that you have no scheduling conflicts. You are not supposed to be at an audition for more than one hour (and if you are, the union requires you be paid a pro-rated day's pay), but you never know what will happen. You do not need the stress of being late for something else while you're trying to focus on your audition. Make arrangements to have your children picked up, etc. Once you're at an audition, you should be able to focus exclusively on your audition.

Do you have a current resume stapled to your headshot in your car? You don't want to show up without your headshot and resume, so put them in your car the day before.

What do I wear?

That seems to be a big question for actors. The best rule of thumb I've ever heard came from Marcia Dangerfield, a talented actress. At a film or television audition, *dress the way the character would dress for a job interview*. In other words, if you're auditioning for the role of a doctor, don't show up in scrubs with a stethoscope around your neck. Wear a suit. What you want to do is give-off the overall aura of the character, not play dress-up. For commercial auditions, however, you may sometimes need to be a bit more blatant in your presentation.

The day before your audition, check on the obvious because the obvious has lost a role for more than one actor. Is there gas in your car? Did you set your alarm clock? If you need glasses to read, do you have them with you?

Last, but not least, be confident! Get a good night's sleep and prepare yourself to show us the wonderful actor you are!

CHAPTER EIGHT

ARRIVING AT THE AUDITION

This is It!

Because of your good preparation, you're now at the audition rested, dressed right, and on time. That's a good start for a strong audition.

As you get to the audition, sign in. A union sign-in sheet is quite involved, but please take the time to fill it in right. The casting director will greatly appreciate it!

PRODUCER: _____
PROD'N CO: ___HARVEST ENT.___
PROD'N OFFICE _____
PHONE # ___(000) 000-0000___
AUDITION DATE: ___5/6/--___

CASTING REP. NE: _____
PRODUCTION TI...: ___TEX MURPHY___
EPISODE: _____

Casting Director's Signature

CASTING REP:
Please fill in time seen
for each actor

(1) NAME	(2) SOCIAL SECURITY	(3) ROLE	(4) AGENT	(5) PROVIDED?		(6) ARRIVAL TIME	(7) APPT. TIME	(8) TIME SEEN (Cast. rep.)	(9) TIME OUT	(10) TAPED?	(11) ACT. IN.
				PARK	SCRIPT						
JOHN DOE	000-00-0000	TOM	THE BEST	✓	✓	10:30	10:40	10:50	11:00	YES	JD

Next, get your *sides.* If all goes well, you'll be given sides for the character that you're expecting to read for. Don't be shocked, however, if you get sides to a completely different character, because it happens all the time! There are times when I'm casting for relatively small roles, so I have everyone read sides that are actually those of lead characters so I can see how they handle a meatier scene. We may decide, once we see you, that you're actually much better suited to a different role. There are innumerable reasons why you may read a different part than you expected. Let's say that you dressed for the role of a doctor, but you're now reading for a teacher. Aren't you glad you didn't wear those scrubs?

Actors have a tendency to run into people they know at auditions, because they're often going out for the same roles. Don't fall into the trap of playing the social game before your audition. That's your time. Use it wisely! If you just have to touch base with someone, exchange phone numbers and *do lunch* later. Don't sabotage yourself by not preparing correctly. I recommend that actors get to the audition at least half-an-hour before their time in order to prepare.

The actual preparation is a very individual thing. Here, however, are some basics.

- Read through the sides once, as you would a book. Don't focus on your character.

- Find out the physical aspects of the scene. Is it day or night? Is it in a kitchen, a school, or outside?

- What pages of the script do you have? The first thirty pages of a script will tend to be more expository than the rest.

- Read through it again. Do you know how to pronounce all of the words? Do you know the meaning of all the words? If you don't, talk to the assistant. If you feel stupid doing so, better to feel stupid in front of the assistant than the casting director.

- Who are the characters in the scene? What is their relationship to each other?

- Come up with a brief summary of the scene to make sure that you understand what's going on. When I ask actors to do this, they'll typically come up with 'this guy is upset because someone came to the door and said something.' I want you to be able to break it down like this: 'John is upset because his neighbor Jane came over to say that she's run over his cat.' Make sure that you really understand the scene.

- Highlighting. People sometimes highlight their lines, which is fine, if the purpose is to be able to come back to your lines easily after looking up at your scene partner. But do not ignore the other person's lines. You can find out more about your character through the other person's lines than you can through your own. For example, if the other character in the scene says, "Why are you yelling at me?" it tells you the tone of voice with which your character is speaking.

- The right emphasis on the wrong syllable. I've watched actors sit, script in hand, trying to figure out which word(s) will be accented in each sentence. They complicate their lives so, when all they really need to know is the attitude of the character and why they're saying what they're saying.

Good acting is really not acting. It is real. To be real, you must know why you are saying and doing the things you are. Let's say you're talking to your brother in a scene. The phone rings, and you pick it up and speak with someone. When you hang up, you tell your brother, "Aunt Mary's coming to the family reunion."

That's a pretty generic line. Many actors will stew about whether it should be, *Aunt Mary's* coming to the family reunion, Aunt Mary's *coming* to the family reunion, or Aunt Mary's coming to the *family reunion.* Wouldn't it be easier to just figure out whether or not you *like* Aunt Mary?

Here's an exercise. Look at the sentence. Pretend you like Aunt Mary. . .read the sentence. Pretend you don't like Aunt Mary. . .read the sentence. Did you have to think about which word to emphasize? No.

Why? Because you knew what you were saying and *why you were saying it.* This is called **making choices.** You get to choose your attitude towards Aunt Mary and your brother and everything else in the scene.

Actors will say, "What if I choose to like Aunt Mary and my character actually hates her?" If you give a good audition based on your choice to like Aunt Mary, we'll take the time to say, "That was great, but would you try it again, and this time, let's say you really don't like Aunt Mary." Once we know you can act, we'll give you the necessary direction. If you make no choice, there is no scene, no direction...*and no part.*

Remember, there is no wrong or right choice at an audition. Actually, the only wrong choice is no choice.

- It helps to think about what your character was doing half-an-hour before the scene takes place. It will give you some background to make choices from. It will set the 'event.'

- Actors often have trouble figuring out what to do with their hands during an audition. Did you bring a cup of coffee with you to the audition? Does it make sense for your character to be drinking a cup of coffee in the scene. It does? Good. Use it!

- When preparing for an audition, unless you have been asked to do so, do not try to memorize the dialogue. You have so much to figure out about the character and the scene, you don't have time to memorize. It's not the point of the audition. Actors who walk in without their sides seem to do so with a somewhat cocky attitude, like 'I'm so good, I memorized it.' Usually, no matter how well they read it in the hall, they will probably forget a line when they get into the audition. Not a good position to be in. BE FAMILIAR with your lines, however. If we can't see you looking up at the person you're reading with, the whole audition will be a waste of time...

- Don't be a slave to the dialogue. If you miss a word, or accidentally change one in context, that's fine. But don't intentionally change or add to the dialogue. There are two main reasons for this: First, the writer is sometimes present during auditions and she likes her words just the way she wrote them; and second, we like for everyone to come into the audition with the same tools.

- With that in mind, it's also possible to get a part by doing just the opposite. An actress was once auditioning for a dramatic role and the existing dialogue was not working for her at the moment. She asked the director if she could use her own words. He agreed. She got the part. The saying *never say never* applies beautifully to the film business.

- If you object to certain language in an audition, don't change it, just don't use it. If your line is, "I hate that damned dog," you could get away with "I hate that dog," but not "I hate that dang dog.."

- Enter laughing. Well, not exactly. But remember, people often laugh at the strangest times. We laugh when we're happy, we laugh when we're being sarcastic, we laugh at ironic situations, we laugh when we're angry. In some strange way, finding some reason why your character would laugh or chuckle brings an element of reality to a scene. I'm not saying to make your reading contrived by very obviously putting in a 'ha-hah-hah,' but if the spirit moves you, do it readily!

  •Be comfortable enough with the scene to be able to use the room when you get into the audition space. Unless you are told to stand in one place for some reason (such as taping), the more you realistically use the room, the better. Again, it will make the scene more real.

  •If 'real' to you feels like sitting in one place, by all means, sit in one place. When using the room, however, remain real. If your character looks out of a window in the scene, and there's a window in the room, use the window to look out of, not the wall. (You'd be surprised how many actors do that.) Unless you've auditioned in that space before, you won't know what to expect; so just be open and *grounded,* and go where the scene takes you.

• Finally, prepare to have a good time. Breathe. They're calling your name.

Monique Lanier's break!

Monique was a drama student at the University of Utah when Halloween V came to town to shoot. Casting director, DeeDee Bradley auditioned her and loved her work. Monique, being a gentle soul, objected to the basic premise of the script, and really did not want a part, but DeeDee recognized Monique's talent and asked to manage her. Monique agreed, having no idea how very difficult it is to acquire a manager of that caliber.

Soon after completing Halloween V, DeeDee was hired to put the original cast together for the TV series, Life Goes On. Monique was cast as the original Page, and went from being a student to a recognized TV star. Monique is a fabulous actress, and continues to pursue her career. She is also becoming a nurse.

CHAPTER NINE

THE ACTUAL AUDITION

This is your moment, your space, your time to shine!

Walk into that room as though you are making a stage entrance. Remember, you are coming into *your* living room, greeting *your* guests. When you enter the room, make sure that you have your headshot and resume (STAPLED together, bac to back) and sides. In a big, confident voice, introduce yourself (Host!). If you can find it inside yourself, as you are approaching the casting director, and after you've introduced yourself, try to make a warm, honest, comfortable statement that does not require a response.

Making a positive comment can break the ice in an awkward situation (Host!) and not requiring a response will avoid a potentially tense moment. If the casting people are not responsive, think of them simply as being reluctant, shy guests. (Host!) Your warmth and confidence will put them at ease. Take control. Hand the casting people your headshot and resume, but don't attempt to shake hands. If not reciprocated, it will be very uncomfortable.

You are both there for a reason. You are there to audition, and the casting director is there to watch you. Time is of the essence. After you've handed over the headshot and resume, you will pretty much know if the casting director wants to talk to you, or if he simply wants to see you read. If there's any lull at all, take control graciously (Host!), and announce that you're ready if he is. Never, ever give the audition a negative tone. Don't tell them "I'm sorry I don't look better, but my agent reached me at the gym and I didn't have time to go home," or "Parking is horrible out there." Any negativity out of your mouth will drag down the mood of your audition. During this brief period, you should have had time to scope out the room for your blocking.

Just about every actor walking into that audition will be able to create a picture of the scene for the casting people by connecting the dots like we used to do in our first-grade workbooks. They'll be able to deliver the lines in the right order. They'll be able to give the basic interaction necessary to the scene. But the actor that gets the callback and then, the part will do something more than that. He'll create a Van Gogh. He'll color outside the lines. He'll fill in the dead spots. If you set up a still life on a table and in some miraculous way were able to gather VanGogh, Rembrandt, Matisse and Picasso and tell them to paint that still life, you would have four wonderful-but very different - paintings. If, in the same sense, you handed the same script to Jack Nicholson, Danny DeVito, Mel Gibson and Samuel L. Jackson, you would get four wonderful- but very different interpretations. The script is only the *still life*- what makes it *art* is what you bring to it.

If the scene requires you to read with someone, it will happen in one of three ways: The casting director will read with you, a reader will read with you, or you will read with another actor. The worst situation, usually, is the first. Casting directors often don't give much in a reading and may spend time looking at the page when they should be watching you. Remember, as much importance, if not more, is placed on what you're doing when your character is not speaking. You should be listening to what the other person is saying to you.

The key to a good scene is listening. If you listen to someone say something that makes you angry, you will avoid thinking, *this is the part that makes me angry. I should look angry.* If such thoughts go through your head, it will look like you're acting, whereas, if you truly *become* angry because of the words said to you, the scene will become real.

Many actors are afraid to make eye-contact with their scene partner, because they might lose their place when they return to the page. If you slide your thumbs to your next line each time, you will always know where you're supposed to be.

If you read with a reader or another actor, the best thing that can happen to you is to read with someone stronger than you, because they will pull you into a scene. It will become magic. You will sometimes be teamed-up with someone before you step into the room, but it will more likely happen at the last minute. Go with the flow. Don't worry if the other actor isn't quite on the same track you are. Are our day-to-day conversations so rehearsed that we know how the person we're speaking with will always respond? No. Go with it.

Unless there is a key point in the sides that you just can not figure out, or are completely befuddled, avoid asking questions. Part of the audition is to see how much you can work out on your own. And when questions are not answered in the sides, it's a great opportunity for you to make interesting choices. Do so.

Unless the ceiling falls in during the audition, DO NOT **break character.** Breaking character means that you stop the scene and come out of character. Breaking character will pretty much guarantee not getting a callback. I've seen actors break character for all sorts of reasons—they flub a word, lose their place, trip on the rug, hear a siren go by. . .

Haven't you ever done any of these things in real life? And when you did, did you stop doing what you were doing and start over? Of course not. So don't do it at an audition, either.

There will be times when you will flub a word, and it will throw you for the rest of the reading. If that happens to you, and you are sure that a second reading will be 100% better, ask to do it again. But this is a risky endeavor. If that second reading is not far, far superior to the first, you have not only wasted the casting director's time, but you've given her the opportunity to see *two* bad readings instead of one, making sure that your 'talents' are deeply ingrained in her mind.

On the other hand, the very best thing that can happen to you is to have the casting director or director ask you to do a scene again, usually with direction. When this happens, you must have given us a good first-read. Following the logic of the last paragraph, we're certainly not going to ask you to read again if your first reading was poor. But if you're asked to read again, **listen to the direction given to you, and follow it**. Often, the purpose of such an exercise is to see if you can, indeed, follow direction.

Because it is your time to prove yourself, if you do not feel ready to read again at the drop of a hat with the new direction given to you, ask to go out for a while to make the adjustment. The answer will rarely be 'no,' since we, too, want you to do your very, very best. Let the casting director see as many people in between as you need, and then come back into the room and knock us out!

After you've read once, you may be asked to read for another role. The same thing applies. Ask to go out into the waiting area. You will need your prep time. Take it. An audition has nothing to do with speed. It has to do with being real.

An important component of a good audition is the fact that you are telling the casting director a story. And like any good story, yours needs to have a beginning, a middle and an end. Look at your sides, see where the three mini-acts are. It will not just make the scene more interesting, but will give you a chance to layer the audition. You'll be able to show us even more than what was in the script. I'll give you an example of this in the upcoming One-Liners section.

Here are a few do's:

- Make eye contact as much as you can with the person who's reading the other character(s).

- Take your time! Don't rush! There are times when a lengthy pause, appropriately placed, can make an enormous impact.

- There are times when your character is cut off by another character. Your line may read something like this, 'What was I trying to say. . . ' If the other person reading doesn't cut you off, it will be very uncomfortable for you. I recommend figuring out (in character) how you will finish that sentence if you are not cut off. This is a legitimate time to add dialogue.

- Remember to have your hair away from your face, and your face and eyes within view of the casting director. The eyes are what we need to see. With that said, it can make quite a dramatic statement to purposely turn your back or hide your face with your hair when doing so for a reason.

- Know the difference between a page number, which is in the upper right-hand corner of the page, and a scene number, which shows up on both the left and right-hand side of the description or dialogue at the beginning of each scene.

53.

CONTINUED: (2)

                    BRITTANY
            Where's the money?

EXT. STREETS - DAY

Joe is driving frantically looking for a street sign. He
glances down at a piece of paper with the words, "2211
LUCKY JOHN DRIVE" scribbled on it.

I/E. TIM'S GARAGE - DAY

Brittany throws the final bag into the back of the Black
Jeep. The bag falls into place adjacent to the Camo Money
Bag and on top of the Dead Body Duffle Bag. She slams the
trunk and hops into the passenger seat. Tim walks briskly
into the garage, shirt half on and hops into the driver's
seat. He turns the ignition and nothing happens.

                    TIM
            (ala Sean Connery)
        I thought you fixed it "Q".

                    BRITTANY
            What was that?

                    TIM
            Bond.

                    BRITTANY
        No idiot.. the engine what's goin' on?

                    TIM
            Don't call me an idiot.

                    BRITTANY
            (pointedly)
        We have to take this car to make our
        plan work. Now, can we fix it?

                    TIM
            Do you have jumper cables in your car?

                    BRITTANY
            (disappointedly)
            No.

                    TIM
            I'll be right back.

Tim hops out of the car and hauls his keester down the
street. Brittany closes the garage door.

And a few don'ts:

- Don't make physical contact with the casting director unless it's initiated by him. If you're reading with him, and the scene calls for you to grab your scene partner's hand, don't do it. Some casting directors abhor being touched, and not touching him will save you from the embarrassment of being told so.

- Avoid changing dialogue.

- Unless requested to do so, or maybe an on-camera audition, don't memorize the lines.

- Unless it's purposely being done to suit the character, never chew gum at an audition.

- If the character calls for an accent, do one. If there is no accent, don't create one. It's going to be hard enough to make your audition real without adding linguistic phonetics to the challenge.

- Screenplays consist of dialogue, which is indented, and scene descriptions which bind the dialogue together. There is often stage direction. Stage direction reflects the imagination of the writer and does not have to be followed step by step in your audition unless that direction has a clear bearing on the scene. For example, the writer has stated that your character is smoking a cigarette. Please do not mime it or worse yet use a pencil. Miming in this particular circumstance is unnecessary and therefore uncomfortable. If, however, your character is not only smoking in the scene, but burns the other character, by all means, you will need to be smoking from the beginning of the scene. The cigarette can't just pop up for that line. In other words, don't mime any action unless you need to do so to make the scene real.

- Songs don't end on the last word. A closing melody gently takes us out. The same thing needs to be done at an audition. Stay in character for at least 30 seconds after your last word, and bring the scene to an end in a natural (real!) way. You should stay in character until the casting director ends the scene by saying "Thank you," or something of that nature.

Everything I've described so far applies to a normal, run-of-the-mill audition, but there are certain other auditions which can be even more challenging.

one·Liners

Sometimes you will audition for the role of a character whose dialogue consists of one sentence, or sometimes, one word! Even though the sides for such roles may seem impossible to develop, they are not. They can still be broken down into a mini-play, just like any other scene. I don't mean for you to turn a one-line audition into five

minutes in fact, please don't do that - but you must make it interesting in order to have a chance at the role.

One of the biggest temptations in auditioning for a one-liner is that you may have a tendency to turn it into Shakespeare. If the line requires a big reading, fine; but it rarely does. Let's say you're a doctor. A patient has been wheeled into the emergency room. You examine the leg briefly, and your one line is "The x-rays will confirm it, but I'm pretty sure it's broken. "

Because the situation may seem somewhat dramatic, actors will have a tendency to deliver the line in a harried, frantic tone. Why? What does the character do for a living? If I went to an emergency room and had a doctor panic at a broken leg, I think I'd take the first ambulance out of town!

Another thing which actors do at one-line auditions is to shrug off the importance of the part. When asked if they're ready, they'll often (quite sarcastically) say, "Yeah...it's only one line." When I hear that, I know I'm probably in for a terrible audition. And I'm rarely wrong in those cases.

Just like in a regular audition, stay in character for a moment, before and after you've delivered the line. Treat the one line of your audition like you would treat any one line in a wonderful, meaty, lengthy monologue. Your line is no less important.

I was once doing the local casting for a movie which opened with a mother finding her two children dead. The mother lived in the woods and left her two children for a few minutes to run to a store to get some milk. It is nighttime when she returns. She walks into the kitchen and calls each of her children. She then sees blood splattered all over the walls and calls her children again. (Lovely, isn't it?) I saw actor after actor after actor, and the scene just never came together. It was dull. It wasn't real. Then Jan Tanner came in.

She started the audition by leaving the room and coming back in through the door of the casting area with her arms full of bags (she'd borrowed things to carry in from the people out in the hall). Keys in hand, she came into the kitchen, flipped on the lights and distractedly called her children as she focused on putting down her load. She then took the time to see the blood. Even though we were in a familiar casting space, I was tempted to look for the blood myself, her reaction was so real. Her second call to her children was blood-curdling. She got the part. The dialogue consisted of four words.

Let me give you a very short scene and show you what can be done with it:

THE BABY-SITTER EXERCISE

A baby-sitter (or parent) walks into a baby's room. When he/she gets to the crib, he/she sees that the baby is missing. He/she calls 911.

>   She was just here a minute ago..Yes,
>   I'd like to report a missing child.
>   Almost two years old. . .
>   3822 Johnson Road. Hurry!

What are the beginning, middle and end of this scene?

Beginning: The person walks into the room to check on the child.

Middle: He/she looks in the crib, realizing the child is gone.

End: He/she calls 911 for help.

What choices need to be made for this scene?

Are you a baby-sitter or a parent? Remember, there are no right or wrong choices. I'm not looking for the right answer, here. I'm asking for you to think this through enough to understand which choice would be more interesting for you. What would the difference be between a parent and a baby-sitter? A parent would be more familiar with the child's habits, would be accurate about the child's age, and would know the address immediately. A baby-sitter may not have all that information on the tip of his tongue. What difference would this make to the scene? Well, if the baby-sitter wasn't sure of the address, it would give the actor an extra layer looking for the address. This may make the scene more interesting and probably more intense for the person(s) watching.

What were you doing before you came in to check on the child? If you make no choice here, the beginning of the scene may be awkward for you. If you were reading before you came in, walk in holding an open book. If you were sleeping, there may be a bit of a stretch. If you were doing dishes, maybe you have a dish towel. Okay, you probably won't have a dish towel at an audition, but I'll bet you could get your hands on a book. By making such a choice, the person(s) watching the scene can tell, 'Okay, this person was reading and now they've come in to do something.' It adds reality to the entire setting. *You have set the event.*

You may be able to think of several other choices that you would need to make for this scene, but let's take it act by act and see what more can be done with these sides:

Act I (beginning)

The character is walking into a room. Why not actually walk in the door? Establish where the crib is and walk to it quietly. Remember, you're checking on a sleeping child. Don't over-do the tip-toeing. That's not real. Just be quiet. Remember, throughout this audition the casting people will need to see your face. What is the character's mood? There's no panic, yet. Don't anticipate. There is nothing wrong. You are simply checking on a child.

Act II (middle)

You get to the crib. The child isn't there. Look for the child. Look in the crib, and then look around the room. Think realistically. If you were in this situation, would you really panic immediately? I hope not. Any two-year-old is capable of getting out of a crib. So look around the room.

You could even make another interesting choice at this point. Maybe you imagine the child is playing hide and seek. If you made this choice, we would get to see a playful side of you. After a few seconds of the play you could begin to be truly concerned. The transition period would be a great time to deliver the line, "She was just here a minute ago. . ." because the line is really not meant to be delivered to 911. Let your mood shift: from puzzled to playful to concerned (or maybe panicked).

Act III (end)

Do anything but pick up an imaginary phone out of thin air in the middle of the room and start talking into it. This will not look real. The very best option is to use a real phone. Did you bring a cell phone? Is there a phone in the room? (Ask to use it first, though.) If there are no real phones in sight, then go to a real wall and take the phone off the wall. This will look far better than taking it from mid-air.

The standard actor phone is created with the hand clenched and the thumb and pinkie extended. Try that. Then, try just clenching your fist and holding it to your ear. Which looks more real?

The next step is to dial three digits. (Many actors have a magic phone that automatically dials 911 when they pick it up.) Remember, too— that *911* is only three digits, not six or eight.

After you've dialed, give the operator time to answer. Listen to her asking you the questions before you answer. Remember, if you're a sitter, you may not know the address off-hand. Look through a pile of papers until you find the address. At the end of the dialogue, hang up. If the casting director doesn't stop the audition immediately, keep looking for the child for another ten to fifteen seconds.

Do you see now how much can actually be done with what initially appeared to be a very simple, short scene? Treat a one-liner the same way you would any other audition. The dignity you lend to it will reflect well on you.

On-Camera Auditions

There are two types of *on-camera* auditions: One—used as a reference tool only, where the actor doesn't have to concern himself with anything but the audition and; Two—where the actor walks in, hits a mark, sometimes looks right to the camera, and reads his lines.

The first kind won't inhibit an actor, the second kind probably will. These are tough. Even the best actors have trouble with on-camera auditions, and as a casting director, I despise them. I feel they serve the purpose of showing us what you really look like (as opposed to some headshots), but beyond that I find them pretty worthless for a number of reasons.

- The person watching the tape will not get the feeling of the actor, which you can only get in person.

- A good audition is one in which the actor can express himself through the use of the room, through unrestricted movements that tell the story. He can't do that and stay in *frame.*

- An actor has to think about where the light is hitting his face, the angle of the camera—things he shouldn't have to deal with at a first audition.

Now that you know why I dislike them, what do you do when you go to a taped audition? For one thing, know what your frame is. Your frame is the perimeter of what the camera can see. Knowing the frame tells you how restricted your movement needs to be if you want your audition to show up on the tape.

Like on a set, don't begin your audition until someone has said action! This means that the camera is rolling. You will probably be asked to *slate* at this point. To slate you look right at the camera lens and say your name, sometimes your agency and the role you're reading for. If the casting director asks for you to name your agent, don't say, "Tom." (Don't laugh. It happens all the time.) What we want to know is the name of the agency, not the name of your *agent.*

After you've slated, take a second to get into character. It is important that we know who you are when you walk into the audition, not the character. At the auditions for *The Crow: Salvation,* a young actor walked into the room for an emotional audition in character. She was shaking and on the brink of tears. I knew her as a person, but the director didn't. And he never got to see anyone but an emotional wreck. Director Bharat Nalluri is a wonderful, kind man—and a joy to work with. But for this actor, his written comment next to her name when she walked out was: *Psychotic.* She obviously did not get the part. We must see *you*, no matter how short a time it is before you do get into character.

Then, begin the scene. If you're reading with someone, you might be confused about where to look. Should you look at the person you're reading with, or just read to camera? This is a question you should ask before the camera rolls. A polite reader will stand right next to the camera, so that talking to camera will be natural—but be prepared. Sometimes, you have to read to camera while the person you're talking to is standing right next to you.

An on-camera audition is the one exception where your sides should be as memorized as possible. If you look down even slightly while on-camera, it will look like your eyes are closed. Have those sides in hand if you need to look at them, but avoid doing so as much as possible.

Develop the scene the way you would normally, but keep in mind that you'll need to restrict your movement. Treat the camera like the person of your dreams. In most any kind of scene, the camera can be dealt with flirtatiously. Manipulate. Demand its attention. Even in an angry scene, the camera should replace the object of your anger—anger being just another expression of passion. When you love the camera, something in your eyes will bring out the life we need to see.

Here's the key to a great on-camera audition: As much as an actor hates on-camera auditions, what does he pray for once he gets the role? *A close up!* **And what's the difference?**

When you get your sides for the audition, work them in a full space. If you're working them at home—use the upstairs, the downstairs, the backyard—whatever you need to make the scene live and breathe. Really learn what it's about. Find every emotional layer. Accept every nuance of the character. Now that you know what the scene is about, you are ready to convert your performance into an on-camera audition.

Take everything you know about the scene, and internalize it. Everyone of those nuances that you found when you were working the scene throughout your house can be brought in and used in a *close-up* frame. And at this point, do not let that frame keep you from being real. Even though the bulk of the performance has to be facing camera so that we can see your eyes, it doesn't mean that you can't turn around for a second. If the scene involves you looking for something—really looking, we need to see you look behind you. Make the scene real!

Remember that for on-camera auditions, you must *color outside the lines*—break out of the box—you restrict yourself far more than the camera restricts you. Don't do that! Enjoy your close up!

Just as in a regular audition, do not break character at the end. Avoid saying 'scene,' as many actors do to indicate they've finished. I personally find it to be jarring and unnecessary.

Improvs

Improvised audi-
tions are usually
only used for com-
mercials, but there
are exceptions. In an
improv, you will be
given a situation,
and you will develop
a story around that
situation. I've men-
tioned that at most
auditions you will
need to become an
actor/director. At an improv audition, you will need to become an
actor/director/writer. At some improvs, you will be asked to just act
something out with no dialogue. At others, you'll be free to speak.
The speaking ones tend to be a little easier.

One of the funniest things I've ever seen happen at an audition was
an improv. Chrysler was auditioning all over the country for the perfect young American family—mom, dad and two kids. All of the
auditions were put on tape to be sent into the ad agency. At my audition, I set up four chairs to look like the front and back seats of a car.
I took actors as they came in—a man, a woman, two children. When
I got to the end of the day, there were three children and one man left.
None of the children looked too pleased about being there, and
improv certainly was not their thing.

I gave the actors the suggestion that they were leaving the car lot in their new Chrysler. Because dad just got the car he wanted, he's taking the kids to get an ice-cream cone.

The camera rolled and the actor gave his all to get the kids to respond enthusiastically about the new car, all to no avail. He tried everything. It didn't work. No matter what prompting he initiated, the kids sat, stone-faced, giving nothing back. The actor finally looked point-blank at the child seated next to him and said, "What do you think of our new car?" Without blinking, the child responded, "It sucks." Somehow this actor had the savoir-faire to look right at the camera and say, "We should have bought a Chrysler!"

The Callback:

For God's sake, don't say 'yes' until I've finished talking!

·Darryl Zanuck

Especially at a callback, you can expect to get some sort of direction from the director. It may be totally contradictory to what the casting director told you at the last audition. It happens. Don't be so nervous and anxious to prove yourself that you rush into the second reading without knowing what the director really wants. If her direction isn't clear, ask for clarification. And if you need time to work on that direction, take it. This is your only chance.

Just like in the first audition, you may be asked to read for a different part. This is a great sign. Take your time and enjoy the experience.

You've had the callback. Now, how is the decision made?

If the casting director did her job right, it's unusual for a director to really dislike any of the actors she sees at a callback. It may become a question of who brought the most interesting choices to the role, or it may be just a physical look. For example, if the lead actor is 60, and we're casting the role of his ex-wife who has three scenes with him, we will probably try to cast someone who is a good physical match. If three actors are finalists for the role of the ex-wife, and the director likes all three of them, she'll probably look to match physical attributes. If one of the actresses is 50, another 57, and the third is 61, the role will probably go to the 57 year old actor. Sometimes, it can actually come down to that.

Who has the actual say on casting? The director. Why is so much importance placed on the casting director?

A casting director can receive thousands of submissions for a project. Of those thousands of submissions, she will probably narrow auditions down to maybe two hundred actors. Of those two hundred actors, the casting director may bring in 40 people to see the director. And at the callback, the director usually pays close attention to the casting director's intuitions. Yes, the director makes the final choice, but can you now see the importance of the casting director's role?

As a final word, don't be too discouraged if you don't get the part. Having gotten a callback means you are now a contender. It's only a matter of time before you get a part. Hang in there, train, and stay positive. Consider this note that was written about Fred Astaire after his first audition.

Fred Astaire

"Can't act, can't sing, slightly bald. Can dance a little."

CHAPTER TEN

DON'T CALL US, WE'LL CALL YOU

It's an Honor!

You've heard actors say that they didn't really mind when they weren't the winner of the Academy Award. "Just being nominated by my peers," they say, "is a great honor." The same can be said of a callback. Okay, so you don't get paid to go to a callback, but other than that, you should feel ecstatic just to get one. Not only do you have a shot at getting the role for which you auditioned, but the casting director obviously likes your work and will be open to bringing you in to read for future projects.

My philosophy on callbacks is: If it ain't broke, don't fix it! In order to get a callback, you obviously did something right, so do what you can to repeat that performance. I even go to the extent of telling people to wear exactly what they wore the day of the first audition.

Unless it's absolutely imperative for, say, another role, do not cut or color your hair or change your look in any way between the audition and the callback. That one change could lose the part for you.

The callback time which you're given will probably allow for a bit more time than you had the first call. Even though, at this point, you may already be out three headshots and resumes on this project alone, you still need to bring yet another one to the callback. The casting director may end up not needing it, but it's always better to be safe than sorry. Chances are, the director will be at the callback. You've already made a good impression on the casting director, but don't let your energy dwindle. You still have to make that same great impression on the director. Follow all of the guidelines which I've given you on making an entrance. Remember, you're still the host!

I've had agents call me after the completion of the first auditions to tell me that one of their best actors was out of town, but is back now, or they have a new actor in the agency who is perfect! Please see him! It goes against every grain of good sense for a casting director to bring an actor in to see a director when they're not familiar with the actor's work. Of course, the agent will say he's terrific. What else are they going to say?

I once gave in to such an agent and brought a young girl into a callback to read for the part of someone in labor. The MOW was *Siege at Alta View,* about a man named Richard Worthington (played by Harry Hamlin) who held a group of people hostage in a hospital after he'd killed a nurse. The true story revolved around the mother-to-be who was the first person in America to give birth in a hostage situation.

The actress came in and read for not just me, but the executive producer, the writer, the producer, the CBS casting executive and the director. Her entire audition was delivered in a squeaky, monotone, dreadful voice. As her audition progressed, I squirmed, sliding further and further down my chair. When she walked out the door, I saw the demise of my career flashing before my eyes as the people in the room sat motionless. Peter Levin, the director of the project, and luckily an absolutely charming man, looked at me and said, "If we cast her, the audience will be rooting for Worthington to shoot her."

The moral of the story? Don't beg your agent to get you into a callback if the casting director did not request you. It won't happen (*or it shouldn't!*).

After a callback, the decisions are made. There are innumerable ways this can happen: You were terrific in the role; you were a good physical match for the other actor in the scene; you had a special skill; you were available on the right dates; you fit the period clothing. . .

Whether you get the role or not, don't second-guess the process. It will just drive you crazy and serves no good purpose. If you get a role, you'll hear from your agent. If you don't get the role, pat yourself on the back for getting a callback, and look forward to reading for that casting director again.

CHAPTER ELEVEN

THAT LONG-AWAITED CALL FROM YOUR AGENT

Walt Disney

Walt Disney was once asked what it was like to be a star. " It feels fine," he said, "when it helps me get a good seat at a football game, but it never helped me make a good film, or a good shot in a polo game, or command the obedience of my daughter. It doesn't even seem to keep the fleas off our dogs and if being a celebrity won't give one an advantage over a couple of fleas, then I guess there can't be much in being a celebrity at all."

Here's the real moment of truth. Your agent calls. You got the part!

Be clear on the scheduled shoot date, what part you're playing, and if you've been given any other specifics about the character. You should get a script within a couple of days. Production is often quite hesitant to give the actor shoot dates and for good reason. If we quote you a shoot date, you are legally entitled to hold us to that date.

What happens if you're quoted February 6th as your shoot day, and the film runs into horrible weather which delays production? If you don't shoot until, say, February 9th, production will have to pay you for the 6th, 7th, 8th and 9th. That's why you may not know your shoot date until the very last minute. The next-best thing to an actual shoot date is an on-or-about which gives production a 24-hour leeway on either side of the shoot date (this is only applicable to weekly players).

This is also the point at which you should confirm your rate, or find out how much money your agent has negotiated for you. As actors become better-known, other things are also negotiated: Points, billing (where and how your name will appear in the credits; the best, and very hardest to get, being before the title) or dozens of other compensations. Will you get paid ads? (Will your name appear on posters and other ads?) Will you have your own motor home? Do you get to keep your wardrobe? How much is your per diem if you're shooting on location? Can you have your own make-up artist? These negotiating points are quite a ways down the road. That's not to say, however, you won't reach them, eventually.

Let me break another preconceived notion. Actors seem to think that between the time they get the call and the time they actually show up on the set to act, there will be rehearsals, dinner with the director and socializing with your co-stars. Wrong. If you are one of the leads in a project you will have rehearsal, but otherwise it will most likely go something like this:

You get a call from your agent on March 1, saying you got the part. Your agent tells you you're scheduled to shoot on April 6. Assuming there's no change in schedule, you will not hear what time you are supposed to be on set until April 5 - and often quite late in the day.

It's impossible to tell an actor in advance what time he's supposed to be on set, because the call times for any day will depend on the wrap time the night before. Not until wrap can the AD add-in the time both cast and crew will need for an acceptable turn-around and know what time the next shoot day can begin. When the AD finally calls you, she will give you your call time. It's your responsibility to be at the set at that time, so be sure the AD gives you good directions to the set before you hang up. Films can be shot in some pretty remote areas. Also, find out where you are supposed to park. If you're filming for several days, find out what scenes are being done first so you can prepare the right material.

The AD may also tell you you're *on hold* or you're a *will notify.* *Hold* means that you are being paid for that day, but at this time, are not scheduled to shoot. *Will notify* means that you are being paid for that day and will probably work, but they're not bringing you in first thing. If you are on a *will notify,* it is extremely important that you stick close to your phone, since the AD will be calling you with about two hours' notice. If she can't reach you, it will make her quite nervous!

Colored Pages

If you don't know what they are, you need to learn, so listen up! The film industry has been around for a long time, and we've come up with some wonderful systems to keep things efficient and concise. *Colored pages* is one of those systems. Keep in mind, when a crew is hired, each person sets off in her own direction to do the necessary pre-production work. Few people actually work out of the central office, so it's hard to keep track of everyone.

When a script is first written, it is copied onto white paper and distributed to the cast and crew. But scripts often undergo rewrites until the last day of shooting. Imagine what chaos this could create.

Let's say that a scene calls for two lead actors to be out on the golf course. When the film is cast, the director realizes that neither lead actor golfs, but they both ice-skate. The script is rewritten, and the lead characters are now ice-skating in the scene. How many departments are affected by this change? Locations—they need to cancel the golf course and find a skating rink. Props— no more golf clubs, but ice-skates are needed. Wardrobe—the clothing the actors wear in the scene will be significantly different. Casting—different extras in different clothing. It goes on and on. So how does production keep track of who's received rewrites?

Every rewrite is copied onto a different color of paper. The list of colors is consistent throughout the industry so there's no confusion. The first rewrite has all the appropriate pages copied onto blue paper, the next one onto pink, and on down the line. This way, each department can simply call the production office to find out which color the script is on, and they know if they have all the current rewrites.

How does this affect you, the actor? Imagine having a long monologue which you've spent over a month memorizing. When you get to the set, you find out your monologue was drastically rewritten three weeks ago. Yikes! To avoid this situation, have your agent call the production office a couple of days before you shoot to make sure you have the most current rewrite.

Wardrobe

Besides the AD, the only other person you'll probably hear from before the actual shoot will be someone from the wardrobe department. They will want to meet with you to confirm what you'll be wearing. They'll either have wardrobe which needs to be fitted, or they'll figure out which of your own clothes you'll wear. There is a chance, if you're wearing your own clothes, that they will establish over the phone what you need to wear. When this is the case, you'll probably be asked to bring three outfits. Make sure that you have the appropriate shoes and undergarments to go with each change. Your clothes also need to be clean.

When you get to the set, wardrobe will ask you to change into your set wardrobe. However they dress you is how you are to remain during the entire shoot. Do no rearrange the collar, add a belt, take off a scarf, etc. Wardrobe won't interfere with your acting, so please don't interfere with their job.

It's crucial that you take care of your wardrobe during the shoot. This means either changing or protecting the clothes well during lunch, watching for continuity in each on-camera take, and hanging up your full wardrobe on a hanger at the end of the day. If you are wearing your own clothes, don't take anything home overnight. There's a chance you'll forget something, which would put you in a real bind the next day. You will receive a wardrobe allowance for using your own wardrobe, but you will only be paid for the clothes you wear, not for all of the clothing you bring.

Hair and Make-up

Men and women, unless told otherwise, should show up on set with their hair clean and no make-up, except, maybe base. Women who wear make-up to the set cause the make-up people to work a lot harder, since they'll have to remove all existing make-up before they can even begin to apply what's needed for camera. Just like with wardrobe, do not change your hair and make-up, and be aware of continuity problems.

The Day Before You shoot

Here's the checklist:

✔ Do I have the right script and know the right lines?

✔ Is my wardrobe clean and hanging in the car?

✔ Do I have the right shoes and undergarments to go with the clothes?

✔ Is my hair clean?

✔ Do I have gas in my car?

✔ Do I have the address of the location, and do I know how to get there?

✔ Is my alarm set correctly?

✔ Do I have my I-9 information in the car?

✔ Have I canceled any conflicting appointments?

✔ Are my children/animals/business taken care of?

Now that you're totally prepared, relax and enjoy this wonderful journey. Do your job, have fun, but don't develop a superior attitude. You're acting. You're having fun. You're not curing cancer.

Part III:
on the set

CHAPTER TWELVE
FINALLY ON THE SET AS AN ACTOR!

Memorize your lines, and don't bump into the furniture.
·Spencer Tracy

Spencer Tracy

The above statement is Spencer Tracy's well-known advice to working actors.

Because you're prepared, you get to the set on time, which makes you look good, and makes everyone else happy. I once had a first-time actor who had a 7:00 am call time. He wasn't there at 7, and the AD came to me asking why. (How would I know?) Because we were some distance from a phone, I decided to wait awhile before calling. He wasn't there at 7:30 am, and he still wasn't there at 8. By now, everyone was panicked, and he was holding things up.

I drove to a pay phone, called him, and he answered. I knew how excited he was about finally getting a part and just couldn't understand why he was still at home. When I asked him, he said that he had a 7:00am call time. I said, "Yes, and?" to which he responded: "Well, I've been sitting right by the phone, and no one's called." **Know the lingo.**

When you arrive, check-in with the 2nd AD. He will have you sign in, show you where your dressing room is, and let you know when you need to be in hair, make-up and wardrobe. There's always coffee available. If you want some, ask. You should also be given the day's sides, which will be copied at a reduced size so they can be kept in your pocket or easily hidden.

An organized production company should have your contract waiting for you in your dressing room if you haven't already received it through your agent. If you are working on a union project, there should be at least four copies of the contract, one for the production company, one for SAG or AFTRA, one for your agent and one for you. The latter is obviously the most important, because when it comes down to it, you have to look out for number one. Without a contract, you have absolutely no proof of anything.

The contract which you receive will not be signed by the producer. This is done to protect the producer from signing a contract, then having the actor change the rate, billing or conditions. Don't worry. The contract is still binding in that it was initiated and given to you by the production company.

SAG contracts are standard. The only things which you really need to watch for are:

- The correct spelling of your name, the correct address
- The correct social security number, the correct work date(s)
- The correct amount of wardrobe changes
- The correct rate
- The correct billing
- A drop/pick-up date, if it applies.

If you are given a day player contract on day one, then work, say, two more days, you will not be given additional contracts. The contract sets the conditions, and the daily SAG sign-in and sign-out sheets establish your hours.

Just like you needed to spend your spare time preparing at the audition, you should do the same on the set. You probably won't see the director until you are actually taken to the set, which you shouldn't do on your own. Do not leave the area where you've been told to stay, even to go to the toilet, unless you let an AD or PA know. When they need you, they need you immediately and won't want to have to search for you.

You may be taken to the set for a run-through before you're actually done with make-up and wardrobe. During the first run-through(s), you may be working on the blocking with the stand-in instead of the actual actors.

Once you're taken to the set to actually work, make sure that you have all the necessary wardrobe and prop items with you so that no one has to run back and get them for you. Also, try to use the restroom before you're brought to the set, as it may be a while before there's an actual break.

Directors are totally immersed in the film when they work. Because of this, they may not be real chatty on the set and may call you by your character's name instead of your given name. Don't be upset by this. It's quite common.

Because of SAG and AFTRA regulations, you'll break for lunch within six hours of your call time. You will be furnished with what is usually quite a wonderful lunch and have priority over extras in the lunch line. You will be in line with the crew. During lunch, be careful not to drip or spill anything on your wardrobe!

After lunch, the morning process will be somewhat repeated, with make-up and hair touching you up, and wardrobe checking your clothes. You're now ready to work again.

At the end of a scene, different departments may approach you for different reasons. Props may come and get what they've given you, or special effects may have to deal with you. These people are not authorized to tell you what you are doing next. And if they choose to tell you what you're supposed to do next, confirm it with an AD. I've seen prop people mistakenly tell actors they're wrapped because their department happens to be done with them. And I've seen actors listen to those prop people and go home in the middle of the work day. Whoops!

During the course of your work day, do not do anything that you feel you shouldn't be doing. This applies to nudity, stunts, or anything else which you were not told about which you feel compromises your safety, ethics or morals. If you run across such a situation, call your agent to help get it straightened out. If you can't reach your agent, call SAG. But don't call anyone until you've discussed your concerns with the ADs, and have received no satisfaction. Of course, use discretion in alerting the unions. Don't be a prima dona. Everyone needs to work together to make any film. Take this course of action only if you deem it absolutely necessary.

If you are still working six hours after you've come back from lunch, you will be fed again. The first meal on a set is always called *lunch,* even if it is served at 3:00 am. The second meal is called, appropriately enough, *second meal.* Second meal is far less substantial than lunch. Quite often, you'll get pizza.

If you are working beyond the first day, be sure you have a call sheet before you leave the set. This will tell you not only what your call time is, but what scenes you're doing, as well. If you're wrapped before the call sheets come out, either find out what your next day's call time is, or remind the ADs that you will need to be called if your time has not yet been established. It will not be uncommon for you to get a late-night phone call from the ADs, telling you your call time has been pushed back. This is not a sign of a disorganized production. It is just the nature of the business.

Here's an actual call sheet which you should study and learn how to read:

Producers: Bryce Fillmore, Ray Tremblay			

Producers: Bryce Fillmore, Ray Tremblay

Director: Craig Clyde	**"The Long Road Home"**	SUNRISE: 7:05 AM
Line Producer: Robert Reeves	Majestic Entertainment **CALL SHEET**	SUNSET: 8:50 PM
Production Office: Road Creek Ranch Inn		DATE: MONDAY JUNE 12, 1998 DAY 1 OF 12 DAYS
836-2485 (Phone) Room 10	**CREW CALL @ 6:30 AM** **SHOOTING CALL @ 7:30 AM**	LOCATION: "FILLMORE RANCH"

2ND AD: Aquarirlus Inn 425-3311 x 39   *** All visitors to the set must be cleared in advance by the Line Producer***

Order	SET DESCRIPTION	SCENE	CAST	D/N	PAGES	LOCATION				
	***NOTE: CREW SHOULD RPT. TO CHURCH, A COURTESY BREAKFAST WILL BE RDY @ 6 AM						P	1	Producer Bryce Fillmore	o/o
	AND WILL BE SERVED UNTIL 6:30 AM FOR CREW. THE VAN WILL LEAVE FROM BASE TO						R	1	Prod/UPM Ray Tremblay	6:30 AM
	SET @ 6:30 AM! PLEASE BRING YOUR SCRIPTS WITH YOU, THERE WILL BE NO SIDES.						O	1	Director Craig Clyde	6:30 AM
	SAVE YOUR MAP - IT WILL WORK FOR THE ENTIRE SHOW. LEAVE IT IN YOUR CAR!!!						D	1	Line Prod. Robert Reeves	6:30 AM
								1	Asst. Dir. Jennifer Lence	6:00 AM
	EXT COUNTRY ROAD	102 A,C,E,G	1,4,X	D13	5/8	FILLMORE RANCH		1	Set PA Calvin Cory	6:00 AM
	First we see Seth coming in with cattle, then Andy, and Ted bring them in also									
								1	Script Lisa Spencer	6:30 AM
	EXT DRIVEWAY/TACK SHED	102	2,5	D13	4/8		C	1	DP Gary Eckert	6:30 AM
	Jim is looking for Seth, as they wonder where he went, they see up the road						A	1	Cam Op Jason Zimmerman	6:30 AM
							M	1	1 AC TBA	6:30 AM
	EXT GATE TO HAYNE'S FARM	102 B,D,F,H	1,2,4,5	D13	2 2/8		E	1	2 AC TBA	6:30 AM
	The cattle have been brought home, the healing has begun. The End!						R			
							A			
	EXT DRIVEWAY/TACK SHED	47	1,6	D3	5/8					
	The kids arrive back from their ride, Annie goes to check on Babe. Babe is in trouble...						G	1	Key Grip Rick Levine	6:30 AM
							R	1	Grip Judd Hilman	6:30 AM
	EXT DRIVEWAY/TACK SHED	50	2,6	D3	3/8		I			
	Murdock pulls up, something's wrong, Annie comes and tells him						P			
							E	1	Gaffer Sam Smith	6:30 AM
	EXT CORRALS	51	1,2,6	D3	3/8		L			
	Murdock goes to see Babe with Annie, Seth comes to tell the bad news						E			
							A	1	Art Director Kee Miller	o/o
	EXT ROAD ON FENCELINE	15	1,2,4,5,6	D1	3 7/8		R	1	Asst. Art/Props Nathan Her	6:30 AM
	Seth meets Jim, Andy, and Annie						T			
							M	1	Key MU/Hair Erin Lyons	6:00 AM
				TOTAL PAGES:	8 5 /8PGS		U			
							H	1	Costume Desigr Glen Raisl	o/o

NO.	ACTOR	CHARACTER	STATUS	MAKE UP	SET CALL	REMARKS				
1	T.J. Lowther	Seth George	SW	6:30 AM	7A	RPT. @ 6:30 A	W	1	Asst. Mary Lyons	Per/Erin
2	Michael Ansara	Murdock Hayes	SW	7:30 AM	8A	P/U @ 7:20 A	D			
4	Al Harrington	Andy Larnebull	SW	6:30 AM	7A	COURTSEY P/U @ 6:20 A	S	1	Mixer Doug Cameron	6:30 AM
5	Craig Clyde	Jim Jacobs	SWF	7:30 AM	8A	RPT. @ 7:30 A	N	1	Boom Al Green	6:30 AM
6	Mary Elizabeth Winstead	Annie Jacobs	SW	9:30 AM	10A	RPT. @ 9:30 A	D			
							O	1	Transpo Mario Moreno	o/o
		ATMOSPHERE					P		Wrangler Lamont Christen	6:30 AM
							E			
1 ATMOS - CHARLES HUTCHENS (TED LAMEBULL) RPT. @ 6:30 AM							R	1	Stills Craig Feller	o/o
							A			
		ADVANCE SHOOTING NOTES					T			

EXT MOUNTAIN ASPEN AND PINE	79, 79A	1,2	D9	2/8	ZEDD'S MEADOW	I	O
EXT LOWER MOUNTAINS/FREMONT RIVER	77	1,2	D9	1 4/8		N	
EXT ZED'S MEADOW	89	1,2	D11	1 2/8		S	
EXT LOWER MOUNTAINS	90	1,2	D11	2/8			
EXT MOUNTAINS	91	1,2	D11	2/8		C	1 Chef/Craft Judy Darby	o/o
EXT HIGH MOUNTAIN RANGE	100		D13	1/8	OX SPRINGS	A	1 Asst. Jeremy Yetter	o/o
EXT OX SPRINGS	76	1,2	D9	3/8		T	
EXT HIGH MOUNTAIN RANGE	99	1	D13	1/8		E	X Breakfast Rdy @ 6:00 AM
EXT CAMPSITE #2	93	1,2	D12	3 7/8	CAMPSITES	R	30 Lunch Rdy @ 12:30 PM
EXT CAMPSITE #2	92	1,2	D11	6/8		N	Dinners Rdy @
						G	

NOTES:

Livestock - Andy's Horse, Cattle, Seth's Horse, Ted's Horse, Annie's Horse
Props - Loaded for Cattle Drive, Sling and bandages, Gun w/Scabbard (Does not Fire) Spreader loaded w/manure, Seth's Knife
Vehicles - Hayne's Truck, Jacob's Truck, Tractor w/spreader
Makeup - Tears Sc. 51
Wranglers - Cattle/Horse Rpt. @ 6:30 AM

2nd Unit - Will work all day as "B" Cam

Asst. Director: Jennifer Lence	Line Producer: Robert Reeves

Your first time on the set may give you the impression that everyone is disorganized and lazy. That's because, at any given time, there are several departments which have nothing to do at that very moment. You will often see crew standing around talking. But while they're talking, other department are working hard. That's how the cycle works. Despite how it looks to a first-timer, every crew member works very hard. They make good money, and they earn every dime of it.

When you're on the set, do your job, and let everyone else do their job. It is not your place to tell anyone what they are doing right or wrong. This applies to props, wardrobe, lighting, make-up—everyone. Even if, as an expert in a given field, you know you're right, it is not your place to tell them. Those departments will not tell you how to act. Make this respect reciprocal.

Your first time on the set will be a memorable one, so enjoy every minute of it. Use discretion when bringing visitors to the set, and do not invite anyone to come have lunch with you unless it has been cleared through the ADs beforehand. Each lunch costs the producer approximately $15.00.

You will probably want to take pictures on the set. It will be fine to take pictures behind the scenes as long as your are not interfering with anything. Before you take pictures of the stars or the set, however, you must get clearance to do so. Many films have publicists who have photographers taking pictures, and they don't want any unauthorized pictures floating around. If you do get clearance to take pictures on the set, never do it while the filming is going on. If you take a flash picture, say "Flashing" as you take the picture. This will let everyone know that the flash wasn't a light burning out on the set.

If you have any questions I haven't answered about what's acceptable on the set and what isn't, ask either an experienced actor or one of the ADs.

Hopefully, your first day on the set will be followed by hundreds and thousands of wonderful days on the set!

Working as an Extra

A team effort is a lot of people doing what I say.   -Michael Winner

In one line, that's about it. Extras are lot of people doing what the AD says.

Besides the information given in the above section for actors on set, let me give you a few tips on being a successful extra. (That means, you don't get kicked off the set and may actually be cast again by the extras coordinator.)

As an extra, it is important to be on time, park where you're supposed to, and have the right wardrobe with you. When you get to the location, sign-in immediately and be sure to have your wardrobe and I-9 information with you. Leave valuables in the car; otherwise, you will probably have to leave your things unguarded while you're working, and production companies are not responsible for theft.

Extras usually don't have access to the craft service table. That's because they can wipe out everything on it in seconds flat, leaving nothing for the cast and crew. Sometimes, there will be an extras' craft service table away from the one for cast and crew. Regardless, you should always have access to water.

When you break for lunch, you will go through the lunch line after the cast and crew. This is not because you're being fed leftovers or are considered inferior. Cast and crew can have as little as one half-hour for lunch, and that half-hour begins when the last cast member has gone through the lunch line. Cast and crew need to get back to work right after lunch, extras don't.

When do you go from being an extra to being an actor?

This is called an' upgrade,' and it happens when you are given specific dialogue to say, and that dialogue is recorded.

The above sentence is extremely specific in its wording. I'll show you why. When I say you are given dialogue, I mean *you* specifically, not a whole roomful of people. If the AD says to twenty extras standing in a room, "When the star walks into the room, congratulate him on his promotion," it will not get you an upgrade. You were not selected *individually*, and you were not given *specific dialogue*. An AD or director may also select you to say some dialogue, but realize before it's recorded that this would constitute an upgrade and take the dialogue away. This would not constitute an upgrade.

If, however, the AD or director pulls you out of the crowd and says: When John walks into the room, shake his hand and say, "I'm really happy for you," you would be upgraded.

What does an upgrade consist of?

If it is a union production, an upgrade means that you are no longer an extra. You are now an actor, and are entitled to all actor percs. Your pay has escalated to actor's pay. You are entitled to meal penalties, overtime, wardrobe allowance - all the good things actors get. This also means that you need to fill out the SAG or AFTRA paperwork and a contract.

For this, you need to follow the same procedure as mentioned earlier. Ask the AD for the paperwork, and if you get no response, call your agent. If you can't reach your agent before the end of the day, call SAG or AFTRA. If the production company does not give you the appropriate paperwork, they risk being shut down by the union.

Is working as an extra the first step toward being an actor?

Although working as an extra will do nothing for your acting career, it will give you an idea of how things work on a set. Agents, especially regionally, will tell you that it is good experience to work as an extra.

Being an extra and working as an actor have little in common. You could compare it to the difference between being an artist or being a house painter. Both take particular skills, and they both deal with paint; but it's certainly not the same job. The risk in working as an extra is that the casting people will tend to see you in that light. This can compromise, in their minds, your integrity as an actor. It *does*, however, teach you how things work on a set.

In LA or New York, don't put extra work on your resume. If you're working regionally it is more acceptable to state extra work, but never try to pass it off as an acting job.

If your goal is to be an actor, and you want to do some extra work to get a feel for being on a set, fine; but I would recommend maintaining a very low profile instead of flaunting yourself as actually being an actor.

Dealing With the stars

Woody Allen was once approached by an excited fan who could say nothing to him except, "You're a star!" "This year, I'm a star, maybe," replied Woody, "but what will I be next year? A black hole?"

Woody Allen

The first time you work with any kind of star is always a memorable one. Sometimes for good, sometimes for bad. I have stressed throughout this book that everyone in the film and television industry is human. Believe it or not, this applies to the stars, too. The best advice I can give is to remember that they are there to work.

If you are an actor doing a scene with a star, you will obviously want to introduce yourself. From that point on, you'll probably be able to read very clearly whether or not a celebrity is open to conversation. Most actors like to prepare for the next scene, but remember, preparing can mean different things for different people. For some actors, it will mean doing exercises. For others, it will mean going over and over their lines. And for some, it means chit-chatting to keep the nerves away. My recommendation to you as an actor is not to worry about the star. Concentrate on your own form of preparation.

If you are working as an extra, the rule of thumb is: Do not talk to the stars. I don't mean to create an us-and-them situation, making them a lot more important. As I have just said, most actors will prepare in some way and that preparation may not be real obvious from your point of view. Imagine if 100 extras all decided to chit-chat with the star before the scene starts? What would that do to their prep time?

Read carefully. Then, reread this book, and train, train, train. I hope to see every single one of you in person at one of my seminars, or better yet, at an audition. You shared your dream with me, and I've shared my knowledge with you. Blend the two.

Remember, we all have dreams. Only the doers turn them into goals. Be one of those people. The best advice I can give you is to be yourself, and enjoy!

(For continued information on what is happening in your part of the country, go to **www.actingacrossamerica.com**.)

Appendix A: THE LINGO

ADR: Automatic digital recording, or additional dialogue recording.

AFTRA: The American Federation of Television and Radio Artists, AFTRA oversees anything shot on videotape, although such a shoot can also be done under the jurisdiction of SAG.

Agent: An actor's representative.

Assistant Director and 2nd Assistant Director: In many ways, these position-titles are misnomers, as these individuals are more set managers than they are assistants to the director. The 2nd AD oversees the PAs, and works directly under the AD. If they belong to a union, it is the DGA. The assistant director is usually instrumental in scheduling the shoot, and when on the set, stays close to the director and DP, making sure that the set is running smoothly. The 2nd AD traditionally handles the actors and their paperwork.

Audition: The interview which an actor goes to to try to get a part.

Back to One: Direction given by the AD after a take. It means to go back to the position which you were in at the beginning of the scene.

Beat: Pause.

Best Boy: Best boys are either part of the grip or electric department. They are the right hand person of the Key Grip or Gaffer.

Big: (see Broad) A term used for actors giving too much of a performance in the interpretation of their scene. It refers to expression, voice levels, and body movement.

Blocking: The layout of the scene where the actors will be and what they will be doing during a scene.

Blue Screen: (sometimes Green Screen) A blank screen which acts as the backdrop to live action. Any background can be laid into the background and give the impression that the live action was really happening in the context of the blue screen. (Example: An actor floating through space).

Breaking Character: Stepping out of the scene which you are doing.

Broad: An exaggerated performance. (Same as big)

Bump: Extra pay, usually for a stunt.

Callback: Coming back to see the casting director or director after having made the first cut during the auditioning process.

Call Sheet: A legal-sized sheet given to cast and crew at the end of the day. It gives the details for each department of what will be happening on set the following day.

Call Time: The time at which you are to be on the set, or in some cases, picked up.

Camera Car: A car upon which the camera is mounted for driving shots.

Camera Left: If you are facing camera, your right. If your back is to camera, your left.

Camera Right: Same as camera left, but reversed.

Casting Director: The person hired by a production company to hire the cast for a film, TV show or commercial.

Cattle Call: (see Open Audition)

Character: A person, sometimes real and sometimes fictitious, in a script.

Colored Pages: Pages onto which script rewrites are copied.

Commission: Percentage of income paid by actors to their representative: If an agent, the amount can not be over 10% if it is a union contract; if a manager, the percentage is unregulated, but is traditionally 15-20%.

Continuity: The element of consistency in a scene. Example: if a woman is wearing a hat, it needs to be the same hat worn the same way for each take.

Coogan Laws: Guidelines created by SAG and named after child-actor, Jackie Coogan, for the work and pay schedules of children.

Cover Set: Set which is always ready for shooting at the drop of a hat. If the crew is scheduled to shoot outside, and it rains, they move to the cover set.

Craft Service: Munchies provided for cast and crew by production.

Cut: What is said at the end of each take to let the camera and sound people know to stop their equipment; also, for the information of the cast.

Day-out-of-Days: Schedule made by AD to who when certain people or things will work on set.

Day Player: An actor or stunt person being paid on a day-to-day basis.

DGA: The Director's Guild of America; the union which oversees director, assistant directors, associate directors, and UPMs for film and TV.

Director: The person who has the creative bottom-line on a project.

DP: Director of Photography

Drop/Pick-up: Term used when an actor is dropped from, then picked-up by payroll; this can only be done when there are ten working days between the drop and pick-up work dates, and can only be done one time per actor, per project.

ECU: Extreme close-up.

Equity: American Equity Association (AEA) stage actors' union.

Exposition: Portion of screenplay explaining the plot development through dialogue.

EXT: Seen at the beginning of a new scene description in a script, refers to Exterior.

Extra: Person, usually in the background of a scene, who has no dialogue.

Favored Nations: An agreement which means that all terms are equal among all actors.

Fire in the Hole: An explosion or gunshot is ready to occur.

Flashing: What is said when taking a flash picture.

Forced Call: Making an actor or crew member come to work without the required turn-around time.

Headshot: An actor's picture.

Hold: When an actor is being paid, but is not working.

Honeywagon: Trailer with rest rooms and dressing rooms.

I-9: Documentation which proves a person's legal right to accept employment in the U.S.

Improv: Improvisation.

INT: (see EXT) Interior.

Local Hire: Someone who lives where the film is being shot, and is therefore not provided with lodging, transportation and per diem.

Location Hire: Person hired to work at a location some distance from where they were hired or reside.

Looping: The process of placing dialogue on soundtrack in post-production, such as actors providing improv dialogue for a crowd of extras.

Magic Hour: The time of day when the sun casts a beautiful light which DPs have referred to as magic; a choice, if brief period of time during which filmmakers love to shoot.

Managers: Actor's representative.

Mark: A place where actors are to stand.

Meal Penalty: Fine paid to actors when not provided a meal after six hours of work.

Miming: Acting out.

MOS: Without sound, attributed to German director who pronounced it, "Mitt out sound."

Off Card: A union actor working on a non-union project is working 'off-card.'

On-or-About: A date which implies three different days, giving production twenty-four hours before and after the on-or-about date to start an actor.

Open Audition: Audition open to the public.

PA: Production Assistant.

Pan: Move the camera horizontally across the scene while filming

Per Diem: Money given to actors and crew when on location to cover the expense of food and other personal incidentals.

Period: Project not set in current time period.

Photo Release: (see Release)

Picture Car: A car being filmed.

Picture Release: (see Release)

Plot: Storyline.

Plus Ten: The 10% commission negotiated by an agent; specifically referring to the 10% added to the base pay negotiated for the actor. (If the job pays only scale, the agent can not take a percentage unless he has negotiated the contract to be on a plus-ten basis).

Producer: Person responsible for the financial bottom-line of a project.

Production Report: Report written at the end of each filming day which states how much film was shot, how much film was developed, how many extras worked, how many hours were worked, and any specific problems of the day.

Prop: An item used by an actor which can be held.

Publicist: A person hired to create awareness of a person or project.

Reel: Compiled footage of actor's various roles.

Release: Legal document releasing producer from liability, usually refers to talent allowing producer to use his or her likeness on film and soundtrack.

Residuals: Payments made to actors on union projects when subsequent sales are made.

Resume: Actor's work history.

Rider: An addendum to any contract.

Right-to-Work: Ability to accept employment without joining a labor union, usually referring to states whose labor codes insure that right.

Room Tone: The sound of the room where the company is shooting; sound people will record room tone to use on the soundtrack.

SAG: Screen Actors' Guild.

Scale: Actors' minimum daily and weekly pay determined by SAG and AFTRA.

Second Meal: The meal served six hours after the end of lunch.

Set: The location where a film is being shot.

Set Dressing: Items placed in the scene to complement the story.

Sides: Scenes read during an audition.

Sign-in Sheets: Sheets provided at auditions to record who was seen, arrival and departure times, etc.

Signator(y): A company which has signed an agreement with a union, agreeing to adhere to tall the rules of that union, whether it be SAG, AFTRA, DGA, etc.

Slate: Identifying yourself on-camera at an audition.

Small: A very subtle performance by an actor.

Sound Stage: A large, soundproofed, open structure designed specifically for filming.

Stand-In: A person who stands-in for the main actor while the lighting and blocking of a scene are being set.

Station 12: Report which a casting director must obtain from SAG before employing one of its actors.

Storyboards: Cartoon-type drawing depicting the action and movement in every scene of a film.

Studio Hire: Union term for actors who work in the same area in which they're hired or reside.

Stunt: Action by actor or stuntman construed to have risk of bodily injury attached to it.

Subtext: The subtleties between the lines of a scene.

Taft-Hartley: The form filled out by the producer or casting director when casting a non-union actor in a film being produced by a union signator; producer or casting director must give specific reasons why preference of employment was not given to a current union member; if in a right-to-work state, the Taft-Hartley can not be denied; if not in a right-to-work state, the union has the option of denying the Taft-Hartley and fining the signatory company.

Take: The attempted shooting of a scene. (It usually takes several takes to get the scene right from the actor, director, cameraperson and sound mixers standpoint).

Telegraphing: Broad charade-type actions used by inexperienced actors to get a point across.

Trades: The film and TV industry's trade journals; specifically, *The Hollywood Reporter* and *Variety*.

Turnaround: Cast and crew rest time, from wrap until next day's call time.

Two-Shot: Camera shot with two people in frame.

UPM: Unit Production Manager.

Voice Over (VO): Voice heard to explain or supplement what's happening in a scene.

Walking Meal: Usually second meal; company doesn't actually stop filming, but food is provided.

Weekly Player: Actor being paid on a weekly contract.

Wide Shot (WS): Camera shot covering the entire scene, opposite of ECU.

Will-Notify: A call given to actors when call time is uncertain; indicates an actor will work, but no specific call time has been determined.

Wrap: Term used to signify the end of the day on a shot, or the end of the shoot itself, as in "It's a wrap!".

APPENDIX B: STATE FILM COMMISSIONS

State Film Commission website addresses are available at **www.actingacrossamerica.com**

ALABAMA:	(800)633-5898	FAX: (334)242-2077
Mobile	(334)434-7304	FAX: (334)434-7659
ALASKA:	(907)269-8137	FAX: (907)269-8136
ARIZONA:	(602)280-1380	FAX: (602)280-1384
Apache Junction	(602)280-1380	FAX: (602)982-3234
Cochise County	(520)432-9454	FAX: (520)432-5016
Flagstaff	(520)774-5118	FAX: (520)774-3883
Globe Miami	(520)425-4495	FAX: (520)425-3410
Holbrook	(520)524-6225	FAX: (520)524-2159
Navajo Nation	(520)871-6655	FAX: (520)871-7355
Page/Lake Powell	(520)645-2741	FAX: (520)645-3181
Phoenix	(602)994-2636	FAX: (602)534-2295
Prescott	(520)445-3500	FAX: (520)776-6255
Scottsdale	(602)994-2636	FAX: (602)994-7780
Sedona/Oak Creek	(520)204-1123	FAX: (520)204-1064
Tucson	(520)791-4000	FAX: (520)791-4963
Wickenburg	(520)684-6470	FAX: (520)684-5470
Yuma	(520)341-1616	FAX: (520)341-1685
ARKANSAS:	(501)682-7676	FAX: (501)682-FILM
CALIFORNIA:	(213)736-2465	FAX: (213)736-2522
Berkeley	(510)549-7040	FAX: (510)644-2052
Big Bear Lake	(909)878-3040	FAX: (909)866-6766
Butte County	(800)852-8570	FAX: (916)891-3613
Catalina Island	(310)510-7646	FAX: (310)510-1646
El Dorado/Tahoe	(916)626-4400	FAX: (916)891-3613
Eureka/Humboldt	(707)443-5097	FAX: (707)443-5115
Fillmore	(805)524-3701	FAX: (805)524-5707
Fresno	(800)788-0836	FAX: (209)445-0122
Imperial County	(619)339-4290	FAX: (619)352-7876
Kern County	(805)861-2367	FAX: (805)861-2017
Long Beach	(310)570-5333	FAX: (310)570-5335
Los Angeles	(213)957-1000	FAX: (213)463-0613
Malibu	(310)456-2489-ext 236	FAX: (310)456-5799
Mammoth	(619)934-0628	FAX: (619)934-0700
Monterey County	(408)646-0910	FAX: (408)655-9244
Oakland	(510)238-4734	FAX: (510)238-2227
Orange County	(714)476-2242	FAX: (714)476-0513
Palm Springs	(619)770-9000	FAX: (619)770-9001

Pasadena	(818)405-4152	FAX: (818)405-4785
Placer County	(916)887-2111	FAX: (916)225-4354
Redding/Shasta	(916)225-4100	FAX: (916)225-4354
Ridgecrest	(619)375-8202	FAX: (619)371-1654
Riverside/San Bernardino	(909)890-1090	FAX: (909)890-1088
Sacramento	(916)264-7777	FAX: (916)264-7788
San Diego	(619)234-FILM	FAX: (619)234-0571
San Francisco	(415)554-6244	FAX: (415)554-6503
San Jose	(408)295-9600	FAX: (408)295-3937
San Luis Obispo	(805)541-8000	FAX: (805)543-9498
Santa Barbara County	(805)966-9222	FAX: (805)966-1728
Santa Clarita Valley	(800)4FILMSC	FAX: (805)259-7304
Santa Cruz County	(408)425-1234	FAX: (408)425-1260
Santa Monica Mountains	(818)597-1036-ext 212	FAX: (818)597-8537
Solano County	(707)642-3653	FAX: (707)644-2206
Sonoma County	(707)586-8111	FAX: (707)586-8111
Temecula	(909)699-6267	FAX: (909)694-1999
Tuolumne County	(209)533-4420	FAX: (209)533-0956
West Hollywood	(213)848-6489	FAX: (301)289-9541
COLORADO:	(303)620-4500	FAX: (303)620-4545
Boulder County	(303)442-1044	FAX: (303)938-8837
Colorado Springs	(719)635-7506-ext131	FAX: (719)635-4968
Denver	(303)640-2686	FAX: (303)640-2737
Fort Morgan	(970)867-4310	FAX: (970)867-3039
Greeley	(970)352-3566	FAX: (970)352-3572
Northwest Colorado	(970)879-0882	FAX: (970)879-2543
Trinidad	(719)846-9412	FAX: (719)846-4550
CONNECTICUT:	(203)258-4339	FAX: (203)258-4275
Danbury Housatonic Valley	(203)743-0546	FAX: (203)790-6124
Southeastern Connecticut	(800)657-FILM	FAX: (860)442-4257
DELAWARE:	(302)739-4271	FAX: (302)739-5749
DISTRICT OF COLUMBIA:	(202)727-6600	FAX: (202)727-3787
FLORIDA:	(305)673-7468	FAX: (305)673-7168
Brevard County	(407)633-2110	FAX: (407)633-2110
Broward/Ft..Lauderdale	(305)534-3113	FAX: (305)524-3167
Ft. Meyers/Naples	(941)498-5498	FAX: (941)498-5497
Jacksonville	(904)630-1622	FAX: (904)630-1485
Key West	(305)294-5988	FAX: (305)294-7806
Miami/Dade County	(305)375-3288	FAX: (305)375-3266
Northwest Florida/Okaloosa County	(904)651-7131-ext 233	FAX: (904)651-7149
Ocala/Marion County	(352)629-8051	FAX: (352)629-7651
Orlando	(407)422-7159	FAX: (407)843-9514
Palm Beach County	(561)233-1000	FAX: (561)683-6957
Polk County	(941)534-4370	FAX: (941)533-1247
Tampa	(813)223-1111-ext 58	FAX: (813)229-6616

Volusia County	(904)255-0451	FAX: (904)255-5478
GEORGIA:	(404)656-3591	FAX: (404)651-9063
Savannah	(912)651-3696	FAX: (912)238-0872
HAWAII:	(808)586-2579	FAX: (808)586-2572
Hilo	(808)961-8366	FAX: (808)935-1205
Kauai	(808)241-6390	FAX: (808)241-6399
Oahu	(808)527-6108	FAX: (808)523-4242
IDAHO:	(208)334-2470	FAX: (208)334-2631
ILLINOIS:	(312)814-3600	FAX: (312)814-8874
Chicago	(312)744-6415	FAX: (312)744-1378
Quad Cities	(309)326-1005	FAX: (309)788-4964
INDIANA:	(317)232-8829	FAX: (317)233-6887
IOWA:	(515)242-4726	FAX: (515)242-4859
Cedar Rapids	(319)398-5009-ext27	FAX: (319)398-5089
KANSAS:	(913)296-4927	FAX: (913)865-4400
Lawrence, Overland Park & Topeka	(913)865-4411	FAX: (913)865-4400
Manhattan	(913)776-8829	FAX: (913)865-4400
Wichita	(316)265-2800	FAX: (316)265-0162
KENTUCKY:	(502)564-3456	FAX: (502)564-7588
LOUISIANA:	(504)342-8150	FAX: (504)342-7988
Jeff Davis Parish	(318)821-5534	FAX: (318)821-5356
New Orleans	(504)565-8104	FAX: (504)565-8108
Shreveport Bossier	(318)222-9391	FAX: (381)222-0056
MAINE:	(207)287-5703	FAX: (207)287-8070
MARYLAND:	(410)767-6340	FAX: (410)333-0044
MASSACHUSETTS:	(617)973-8800	FAX: (617)973-8810
MICHIGAN:	(517)373-0638	FAX: (517)241-0593
MINNESOTA:	(612)332-6493	FAX: (612)332-3735
Minneapolis	(612)673-2947	FAX: (612)673-2011
MISSISSIPPI:	(601)359-3297	FAX: (601)359-5757
Columbus	(601)329-1191	FAX: (601)329-8969
Greenwood	(601)453-9197	FAX: (601)453-5526
Natchez	(601)446-6345	FAX: (601)442-0814
Tupelo	(601)841-6454	FAX: (601)841-6558
Vicksburg/Warren County	(601)636-9421	FAX: (601)636-9475
MISSOURI:	(573)751-9050	FAX: (573)751-7385
Kansas City	(816)221-0636	FAX: (816)221-0189
St. Louis	(314)259-3409	FAX: (314)421-2489
MONTANA:	(406)444-3762	FAX: (406)444-4191
NEBRASKA:	(402)471-3680	FAX: (402)471-3026
Omaha	(402)444-7736	FAX: (402)444-4511
NEVADA:	(702)486-2771	FAX: (702)687-4450
Reno/Tahoe	(800)271-2598	FAX: (702)687-4450
NEW HAMPSHIRE:	(603)271-2598	FAX: (603)271-2629
NEW JERSEY:	(201)648-6279	FAX: (201)648-7350

NEW MEXICO:	(800)545-9871	FAX: (505)827-9799
Albuquerque	(505)842-9918	FAX: (505)247-9101
Las Cruces	(505)524-8521	FAX: (505)524-8191
Los Alamos County	(505)842-9918	FAX: (505)662-8399
NEW YORK:	(212)803-2330	FAX: (212)803-2339
Hudson Valley	(914)473-0318	FAX: (914)473-0082
New York City	(212)489-6710	FAX: (212)307-6237
Rochester	(716)546-5490	FAX: (716)232-4822
NORTH CAROLINA:	(919)733-9900	FAX: (919)715-0151
Asheville	(704)687-7234	FAX: (704)687-7552
Charlotte	(800)554-4373	FAX: (704)687-7552
Durham	(919)687-0288	FAX: (919)683-9555
Piedmont Triad Region	(910)777-3787-ext.7	FAX:(910)721-2209
Wilmington	(910)763-0874	FAX: (910)762-9765
NORTH DAKOTA:	(800)328-2871	FAX: (701)328-4878
OHIO:	(614)466-2284	FAX: (614)466-6744
Cincinnati	(513)784-1744	FAX: (513)768-8963
OKLAHOMA:	(918)381-2660	FAX: (918)581-2244
OREGON:	(503)229-5832	FAX: (503)229-6869
PENNSYLVANIA:	(717)783-3456	FAX: (717)772-3581
Philadelphia	(215)686-2668	FAX: (717)772-3581
Pittsburgh	(412)261-2744	FAX: (412)471-7317
PUERTO RICO:	(809)758-4747	FAX: (401)351-9533
RHODE ISLAND:		
Providence	(401)273-3456	FAX: (401)351-9533
SOUTH CAROLINA:	(803)737-0490	FAX: (803)737-3104
SOUTH DAKOTA:	(605)773-3301	FAX: (605)773-3256
TENNESSEE:	(615)741-3456	FAX: (401)351-9533
Memphis	(901)527-8300	FAX: (901)527-8326
Nashville	(615)259-4777	FAX: (615)356-3074
TEXAS:	(512)463-9200	FAX: (512)463-4114
Amarillo	(806)374-1497	FAX: (806)373-3909
Austin	(512)404-4562	FAX: (512)404-4564
Dallas/Fort Worth	(972)621-0400	FAX: (972)929-0916
El Paso	(915)534-0698	FAX: (915)534-0686
Houston	(713)227-3100	FAX: (713)223-3816
Irving	(214)869-0303	FAX: (214)869-4609
San Antonio	(210)270-8700	FAX: (210)270-8782
U.S. VIRGIN ISLANDS:	(809)775-1444	FAX: (809)774-4390
UTAH:	(801)538-8740	FAX: (801)538-8886
Central Utah	(435)370-8390	FAX: (435)370-8050
Kanab/Kane County	(435)644-5033	FAX: (435)644-5923
Moab	(435)259-6388	FAX: (435)259-6399
Park City	(435)649-6100	FAX: (435)649-4132
Southwest Color Country	(435)628-4171	FAX:(435)673-3540

VIRGINIA:	(804)371-8204	FAX: 804-371-8177
Richmond	(804)782-2777	FAX: (804)780-2577
WASHINGTON:	(206)464-7148	FAX: (206)464-7222
Seattle	(206)684-5030	FAX: (206)684-0379
WEST VIRGINIA:	(304)558-2234	FAX: (304)558-1189
WISCONSIN:	(608)267-3456	FAX: (608)266-3403
Milwaukee	(414)273-2879	FAX: (414)273-5596
WYOMING:	(307)777-3400	FAX: (307)777-6904
Cheyenne	(307)778-3133	FAX: (307)778-3190

For international film commission offices information, contact:

(213)462-6092   FAX: (213)462-6091

Appendix C: SCREEN ACTORS' GUILD AND AFTRA OFFICES

Los Angeles:

5757 Wilshire Blvd., Los Angeles, California 90036
SAG: (323)954-1600
AFTRA: (323)634-8100

New York:

SAG:1515 Broadway, 44th Floor, New York, New York 10036
             (212)994-1030
AFTRA:260 Madison Avenue, 7th Floor, New York, New York   10016
             (212)532-0800

Arizona:	(602)265-2712*
Atlanta:	(404)239-0131
Boston:	(617)742-2688
Buffalo:	(716)874-4410**
Chicago:	(312)573-8081*
	(312)372-8081**
Cleveland:	(216)781-2255**
Dallas:	(214)363-8300
Denver:	(303)757-6226
Detroit:	(810)559-9540
Florida:	(305)670-7677*
	(305)652-4824**
Central Florida:	(407)649-3100*
	(407)354-2230**
Hawaii:	(808)596-0388
Houston:	(713)972-1806
Kansas City:	(816)753-4557**
Milwaukee:	(414)291-9041**
Nashville:	(615)327-2944

Nevada:	(702)737-8818*
New Orleans:	(504)822-6568**
North Carolina:	(910)762-1889*
Omaha:	(402)346-8384**
Peoria:	(309)698-3737**
Philadelphia:	(215)545-3150*
	(215)732-0507**
Phoenix:	(702)265-2712**
Pittsburgh:	(412)281-6767**
Portland:	(503)279-9600*
	(503)238-6914**
Rochester:	(716)467-7982**
Sacramento/Stockton:	(916)372-1966**
San Diego:	(619)278-7695
San Francisco:	(415)391-7510
Schenectady/Albany:	(518)381-4836**
Seattle:	(206)270-0493*
	(206)282-2506**
St. Louis:	(314)231-8410**
Stamford:	(203)348-1308**
Tri-State:	(612)371-9120**

(includes Cincinnati, Columbus, Dayton, Indianapolis, and Louisville)

Twin Cities:	(612)371-9120**
Washington D.C.	(301)657-2560

* *SAG only*
**AFTRA only

Appendix D: RIGHT-TO-WORK STATES

Alabama
Arizona
Arkansas
Florida
Georgia
Idaho
Iowa
Louisiana
Mississippi
Nebraska
Nevada
North Carolina
North Dakota
South Carolina
South Dakota
Tennessee
Texas
Utah
Virginia
Wyoming

Appendix E: THE TRADES

There are many trade journals which apply to actors, but I recommend the following:

Backstage: 1515 Broadway, 14th Floor, New York, NY 10036
    (212)764-7300
Backstage West:5055 Wilshire Blvd., 6th Floor, Los Angeles, CA 90036
    (323)525-2356
Hollywood Reporter:5055 Wilshire Blvd., Los Angeles, CA 90036-4396
    (323)525-2000
Variety: LA: 5700 Wilshire Blvd., Suite 120, Los Angeles, CA 90036
    (323)857-6600

    NY: 245 W. 17th Street, New York, NY 10011 (212)645-0067

Index   Page

Catrine McGregor has cast actors in over 200 motion picture and television projects since 1975. Beginning her education at the Lycee International in Paris, she graduated with honors from the prestigious Loyola-Marymount University in L.A. with a Master's Degree in Education and Film and Television. Since 1975, she has produced several feature films and TV series, including *Small Town*, while casting for a full spectrum of formats, including animated features, IMAX, and CD-ROM.

In *Acting Across America*, McGregor creates a valuable handbook for actors at any point in their career. It's not only packed with inside information about how the business really works; but McGregor has taken an unusually down-to-earth, human approach to the seemingly insurmountable challenge faced by unknown actors all over the country who are wanting to break into a huge and mysterious industry.

Distilling the wealth of information she teaches in seminars and workshops coast to coast, *Acting Across America* instructs as it encourages. Having worked with such celebrities as John Travolta, Kirsten Dunst, Dennis Franz and Teri Garr, McGregor's knowledge and understanding of what it takes to build a thriving career as an on-camera actor is both notable and trustworthy.

ACTING

Across America
in Film and Television

by Catrine McGregor

Illustrations by Alex Buie